God's Unchanging Word in an Ever-Changing World

God's Unchanging Word in an Ever-Changing World

Messages of Hope for Weary Christians

STEPHEN M. DAVIS

Foreword by John P. Davis

WIPF & STOCK · Eugene, Oregon

GOD'S UNCHANGING WORD IN AN EVER-CHANGING WORLD
Messages of Hope for Weary Christians

Wipf & Stock
An Imprint of Wipf and Stock Publishers
199 W. 8th Ave., Suite 3
Eugene, OR 97401

www.wipfandstock.com

PAPERBACK ISBN: 978-1-6667-3575-8
HARDCOVER ISBN: 978-1-6667-9316-1
EBOOK ISBN: 978-1-6667-9317-8

02/10/22

To the memory of my parents, James and Alberta Davis,
both with the Lord they loved and served faithfully,
who with love and prayer never gave up on me,
who rejoiced at my salvation and new life in Christ,
with assurance and in anticipation of seeing them again
in the Lord's time in his presence.

Contents

Foreword

On the evening of December 16, 1973, I had the joy of leading my brother, Stephen Davis, in a prayer of repentance and faith in which he surrendered his life to Jesus Christ. We had journeyed together in rebellion and now we would begin a journey together in serving the Lord Jesus Christ. Educationally, he followed the path that I had taken in pursuing first a bachelor's degree, then two master's degrees and a Doctor of Ministry. He then chose to no longer follow but rather took the lead in obtaining a PhD. I have not yet caught up with him. Out of seminary, Steve successfully planted a church in Philadelphia before being called to churchplanting in France and Romania and eventually to pastoral training around the world. In 2008, as we sat in view of the Eiffel Tower, we talked about the final chapter of our lives and decided that it would be a joy to move back to Philadelphia together and plant a church in the city where we both had come to know the Lord.

I have worked side by side now with Steve for twelve years. Together we have shared the struggles and disappointments of church planting, the ongoing pressures and challenges of living faithfully, and dismay and concern over a society that moves farther and farther away from biblical values. Steve's commitment to biblical truth and his love for the gospel provide both an anchor to hold fast to the authority of Scripture and a rudder to navigate through the vicissitudes of life and ministry. This commitment is evident in the way he lives as well as in his preaching and teaching ministry. Steve is an excellent student of the word of God, a wise and discerning observer of human behavior, and one who is conversant with the world in which we live.

Steve does not write from an isolated ivory tower but as one who has walked the streets of Philadelphia, who has counseled and encouraged those with life-consuming addictions, who has suffered the loss of parents and siblings and friends, who has experienced the joys and sorrows of marriage and raising children, and who has pastored and is pastoring in a world of diversity and depravity. As a brother, a friend, and a co-worker in the harvest, I have watched Steve faithfully pursue his calling to walk worthy of the gospel. He would be the first to admit his own failures and imperfections, yet in the same breath he would extol the grace and mercy of God through Jesus Christ. In 1973 Steve experienced the overwhelming power of the gospel. He continues to experience that power and believes that the gospel is God's saving power to everyone who believes. The good news about the person and work of Jesus Christ continues to affect him and remains at the core of his teaching and preaching.

Though we live in an ever-changing world, we have a never-changing word: Jesus is the same yesterday, today, and forever. This is Steve's message of comfort and hope.

John P. Davis
Lead pastor, Grace Church of Philly

Preface

A DIALOGUE IN THE movie *Enemy at the Gates* has Commissar Danilov responding to Khrushchev's demand for ideas to improve morale. Some officers suggest more of the same, including summary executions. Danilov responds, "Give them hope!" The hope provided centers on one renowned sniper, Vasily Zaitsev. Any hope provided is short-lived. In the end, the jealous and traitorous Danilov sacrifices his life and is shot by the German sniper Erwin Köning, who mistakes Danilov for Vasily, who then shoots Köning. Two months later, Stalingrad is liberated, the Germans surrender, and Vasily is united with Tania when he finds her in a hospital. A story of intrigue, heroism, sacrifice, and death. The war does not end then, the suffering continues, and lasting hope is dashed. Beyond the story, even the young lovers' happiness comes to an end with their deaths. Any human hope is temporary and timebound at best. What we need is a durable, lasting, confident hope. As Christians, we find that in Christ and in God's word. This biblical hope is not simply the desire or wish for something to happen but the firm assurance that God will fulfill his promises.

The first two decades of the twenty-first century have been filled with seemingly unprecedented chaos, terrorism, destructive hurricanes, and, more recently, a lingering pandemic. Hopelessness reigns. People talk about returning to normal, or a new normal, and they fear for the future. We all struggle at times to remain hopeful in a world filled with despair. There are times of illness, grief, and loss, and Christians are not spared all the sickness, sorrow, and pain experienced by others with whom they share brokenness in their common humanity. We neither despair nor place our ultimate hope in science, politics, or medicine. For Christians, who understand that they live in a broken world, there is real hope, an assurance grounded in the faithfulness and omnipotence of God Almighty. This hope is not naïve and does not depend on improving world conditions or a return to any kind of normal. This hope does not promise health, prosperity, and worry-free living during our earthly sojourn. Actually, this biblical hope looks past the present turmoil and future upheavals to a new heaven and a new earth. As C. S. Lewis said in *Mere Christianity*, "A continual looking forward to the eternal world is not (as some modern people think) a form of escapism or wishful thinking, but one of the things a Christian is meant to do."[1] God does not promise that we will not experience suffering, loss, and finally physical death unless the Lord Jesus returns in our lifetime. He does promise that he will never leave us or forsake us, that in his "presence there is fullness of joy; at [his] right hand are pleasures forevermore" (Ps 16:11). We must face the reality that our time on earth is allotted according to God's design for our lives, and we should pray "teach us to number our days" (Ps 90:12). We should progressively look forward with anticipation to that day when we arrive home in God's presence. J. I. Packer went home to be with the Lord in 2020. He wrote on aging and death and affirmed that "God prepares us for our transforming transition by stirring us up to desire it."[2]

The eighteenth-century pastor and theologian Jonathan Edwards and his wife, Sarah, endured great hardship in their lives, including the untimely death of their seventeen-year-old daughter Jerusha. She died from tuberculosis in 1748 after caring for the missionary David Brainerd as he lay dying from the disease. In March 1758 Jonathan Edwards died after receiving a smallpox vaccination. A few days after Jonathan's death their widowed daughter Esther also died. Sarah travelled to Princeton for her orphaned grandchildren, became ill on her return, and died on October 2, 1758, at the age of forty-eight. Before her death she claimed Romans 8:38–39:[3]

1. Lewis, *Mere Christianity*, 134–35.
2. Packer, *Finishing Our Course*, 89.
3. See James, "Uncommon Wife of Revival."

> 38 For I am sure that neither death nor life, nor angels nor rulers,
> nor things present nor things to come, nor powers, 39 nor height
> nor depth, nor anything else in all creation, will be able to separate
> us from the love of God in Christ Jesus our Lord.

Our lives are not our own and are not really under our control. We have been bought with the price of the blood of our Savior (1 Cor 6:20). Since our time is measured, we should seek to live for the greatest good—the glory of God. In doing so, we experience a measure of joy, hope, and satisfaction not found elsewhere. The promise of living in the presence of God for the endless, unfathomable ages to come should cause us to rise up in praise for his free, abundant, matchless, and amazing grace.

Introduction

The renowned physicist Stephen Hawking died in 2018. During an interview he gave in 2011, he was asked about the afterlife. He responded, "I regard the brain as a computer which will stop working when its components fail. There is no heaven or afterlife for broken down computers; that is a fairy story for people afraid of the dark."[1] I'm afraid he was very wrong. With his brilliant mind and the exaltation of human reasoning, he was unable to comprehend spiritual truth. I'm also saddened to realize that without a deathbed conversion he is now in eternal darkness. I recently read a biography of Thomas Edison, another brilliant man, credited with hundreds of inventions, not least the incandescent lightbulb. At the time of his death one of his last comments reported by a pastor hoping to find some religious sentiment was, "If there is a life hereafter, or if there is none, it does not matter."[2] How tragic!

An article in *National Geographic* was written recently about billionaire Jeff Bezos's ride into space and asked the question: Is Jeff Bezos building a future in space for everyone? Or was this an expensive vanity project? I can't answer that because I don't know his heart or motivation.

1. Sample, "Stephen Hawking: 'There Is No Heaven; It's a Fairy Story.'"
2. Morris, *Edison*, 11.

Neither do I know what it's like to have more money than anyone really needs. We're told that as the rocket hurtled toward space, at about 250,000 feet the crew capsule separated from the booster and continued to the edge of the atmosphere. As the capsule climbed, the crew members unbuckled their seatbelts and floated in weightlessness for a few minutes. About ten minutes after launch, parachutes brought the capsule safely back to Earth.[3] Think about that! Millions of dollars spent for ten minutes of experience. Most of us will never have or be able to afford that experience. But we might not be much different in the direction of our heart and what we desire. It's not that we desire too much. We are satisfied with too little. We are satisfied with surviving rather than thriving and with temporary sensations rather than eternal investment. We seek momentary experiences to satisfy deep longings that only Christ can satisfy. Ten minutes in space. Wow! A great experience that lives only in memory and has no lasting, eternal impact. When we live in light of eternity, our hearts are not supremely set on how to increase our comfort or maximize our happiness. Notice I said "supremely." We are citizens here on earth and want to live happy and fulfilling lives. We do have responsibilities, jobs, bills to pay, families to provide for, and illnesses to treat. We need to plan for retirement, take a vacation, and deal with unpleasant people and situations. Yet it's a heavenly perspective we need to drive our desires, to distinguish between those things which are important but temporary and those things that are ultimate and eternal. As John Piper says, "It may not be loving to choose comfort or security when something great may be achieved for the cause of Christ and for the good of others."[4] All people will live somewhere forever. When we believe that we will be engaged in God's mission, we will want people to know our Savior. We will want to worship corporately with God's people. We will be generous with what God has entrusted to us. If this does not characterize your life, then in seeking much in life you are really seeking little of eternal value.

John Piper tells the story about a man and his wife who had two children die from genetic defects. Their daughter died just before her second birthday. Their son lived for two minutes before he died. The children both died within three months of one another. The father tells how he and his wife lived with their son for his entire life, all of two minutes. They never saw him take more than a few breaths, never saw him walk, heard him laugh, or wrestled with him. For several months the father was tormented

3. Drake, "Jeff Bezos Reaches Space."

4. Piper, *Don't Waste Your Life*, 80.

by the question: Why would God create a child to live for two minutes? Many years later, the father was asked to speak at a class reunion. He said, "Life is hard. God is good." Then he told the story of his little two-minute baby. And he gave an answer to the question which had tormented him, Why would God design a baby to live for two minutes? His answer was profound. He said, "God didn't design the baby to live for two minutes. He designed him to live forever."[5]

Regardless of how much time God gives you, he has designed you for eternity, to spend eternity with him. I would venture to say that we don't think too much or much at all about eternity, except maybe when eternity seems closer in old age or in times of sickness. Just as God designed that baby to live for two minutes, he also designed how many minutes you will live. Your minutes are numbered. You know that and the thought might be so uncomfortable that you block it out. Then you realize that in light of an unmeasurable eternity, there's not that much difference between that baby's two minutes and however many years God gives you. Do you pursue your life and ambitions with little thought about how God designed your life? When we begin to understand the truths of God's word and the experience of God's people throughout the ages, we are changed. As Piper concludes, "This life, folks, is not the main thing."[6] As Jesus said, we only get so many years to invest, to lay up treasures in heaven (Matt 6:19–20).

In *The Fellowship of the Ring*, after hearing the dark history of the Ring and the return of the evil lord Sauron, Frodo remarks, "I wish it need not have happened in my time." "So do I," replies Gandalf, "and so do all who live to see such times. But that is not for them to decide. All we have to decide is what to do with the time that is given us."[7]

"*I wish it need not have happened in my time.*" In our own day, we might wish that things were different, that we had been born in another time. But that is not for us to decide. We can decide what we will do with the time God gives us. None of us knows how many more years we have to invest. May these messages from God's word bring hope to the weary, worried, and weak. Let's invest well. We are not home, yet!

5. Piper, "Why Would God Create a Baby to Live for Two Minutes?"

6. Piper, "Why Would God Create a Baby to Live for Two Minutes?"

7. Tolkien, *Fellowship of the Ring*, 48.

1

Seeking a Homeland

Hebrews 11:8–16

> 8 By faith Abraham obeyed when he was called to go out to a
> place that he was to receive as an inheritance. And he went out,
> not knowing where he was going. 9 By faith he went to live in
> the land of promise, as in a foreign land, living in tents with Isaac
> and Jacob, heirs with him of the same promise. 10 For he was
> looking forward to the city that has foundations, whose designer
> and builder is God. 11 By faith Sarah herself received power to
> conceive, even when she was past the age, since she considered
> him faithful who had promised. 12 Therefore from one man, and
> him as good as dead, were born descendants as many as the stars
> of heaven and as many as the innumerable grains of sand by the
> seashore. 13 These all died in faith, not having received the things
> promised, but having seen them and greeted them from afar, and
> having acknowledged that they were strangers and exiles on the
> earth. 14 For people who speak thus make it clear that they are
> seeking a homeland. 15 If they had been thinking of that land
> from which they had gone out, they would have had opportunity
> to return. 16 But as it is, they desire a better country, that is, a
> heavenly one. Therefore God is not ashamed to be called their
> God, for he has prepared for them a city.

THE OPENING OF THE Tokyo Olympics featured the well-known song by John Lennon, "Imagine." The song has a beautiful melody and arrangement. Its lyrics, however, are among the worst you will find in popular songs. We are presented a utopian vision, asked to imagine that there's no heaven or hell, and to live for today in brotherhood. People can imagine whatever they want, but it is not reality. They can even wish for a brotherhood of man, a noble sentiment in itself, but impossible if there is no heaven, no hell, everyone living for today, and no religion. You can live by your imagination or by faith. You can imagine reality as you would like it to be or live by faith in the promises of God. You can die and enter the great unknown either hoping there is nothing beyond, that you will be okay if it turns out that there is a God, or you can die in faith trusting that God has prepared an eternal dwelling place. Consider these words from C. S. Lewis:

> Christianity asserts that every individual human being is going to live forever, and this must be either true or false. Now there are a good many things which would not be worth bothering about if I were going to live only seventy years, but which I had better bother about very seriously if I am going to live forever.[1]

You will live forever, either in God's presence or far from it. Our text speaks about people who were strangers and exiles in the land where they dwelled. They looked past their short earthly existence to the future beyond the grave. The first eleven verses of chapter 11 speak of Old Testament people who lived by faith and end with Abraham and Sarah. Verse 1 tells us that faith is a present and continuing reality. This faith believes that God has done what the Bible tells us he has done and will do what he has promised to do. Those we find in this passage died as they lived. They lived by faith. They died in faith. It is interesting that their failures are not mentioned. These people were faithful but not perfect. Their lives were characterized by faith and they believed what seemed impossible from a human perspective. The phrase "by faith" provides many examples of what it means to live by faith.

When we speak of faith we understand it as "substance" or foundation that in some sense inaugurates in us those things of which we are assured, future realities and the fulfillment of the promises of God (vv. 1–2). Verse 6 tells us that without faith it is impossible to please God. There are realities for which we have no material evidence. We have no hard proof about spiritual realties that everyone would find irrefutable and convincing. Faith enables us to know that these realities exist, and while we might not have any assurance of these things apart from faith, faith does give us genuine certainty. None of us were there at creation. None of us had personal

1. Lewis, *Mere Christianity*, 74.

contact with any of the people mentioned here. We believe these truths by faith. Faith is not unreasonable but is not founded on human reason. According to Blaise Pascal, "What is essential is invisible to the eye . . . The heart has its reasons which reason does not know."[2]

Verses 8–12 speak about faithful Abraham and his wife. Verses 13–16 are an explanation, a parenthesis, followed by Abraham again in verse 17. Verse 13 tells us that "these died in faith, not having received the things promised." Only by faith can we see and grasp these unseen realities and remain steadfast when alternate man-made realities are advanced. Often, we must decide whether to believe God, whom we've not seen, or believe the voices and talking heads of our day, who seem to speak with so much authority and assurance. Many of you are familiar with movies which portray people living in a computer simulation without knowing it. There are several, but the only one I recall watching was *The Truman Show*. As entertaining and unrealistic as that seemed at the time, there are now philosophers who propose that we are living in a simulated reality, that we are self-aware software trapped inside virtual reality. As you know, many people find it laughable to think that there is a personal Creator God who made all things and before whom we will stand one day. So they create alternate realities, often using religious language that speaks of transcendence, something or someone out there that is beyond us.

I think most people are seekers: seekers of pleasure, of truth, or reality, happiness, or seekers of purpose. Of course, there are some who believe everything is random, that life has no meaning and personal gratification is the goal of life. God's people are distinguished by what they are seeking. In verse 14 we find people who make it clear that they are seeking a homeland. What kind of people are clearly seeking a homeland? Are we that kind of people? Is it clear in your life today, in your priorities, in your relationship with God's people, in your witness, that you really are a stranger passing through this world? If you're a Christian, this is the kind of person you want to be.

A PERSON WHO ANTICIPATES THE FULFILLMENT OF GOD'S PROMISES (V. 13–14)

Those who lived by faith also died in faith without experiencing all that God promised. They lived and died looking for the fulfillment of a promise

2. Pascal, *Pensées*, 127.

they never fully experienced on earth. Yet it was so real it enabled them to press on against the current of their surroundings and the pressures of their societies. Compare verses 39–40 which repeat this truth: "And all these, though commended through their faith, did not receive what was promised, since God had provided something better for us and that apart from us they should not be made perfect." Yet their lives were ordered by the firm conviction that God would fulfill his promises. Even in death they looked forward to the fulfillment of God's promises and passed them on to their descendants. "By faith Isaac invoked future blessings on Jacob and Esau. By faith Jacob, when dying, blessed each of the sons of Joseph, bowing in worship over the head of his staff" (11:20–30). For us as well in our present condition, in our mortal bodies, and with our inability to fully contemplate the glory of God, we cannot experience or rightly perceive all that God has promised. We can know that we are saved, that we are forgiven, that we have the promise of eternal life, but we only grasp what is possible to know with our present limitations. This promise has now been fulfilled in Christ. A new age dawned at his coming. We are fellow citizens of the heavenly Jerusalem with all the saints of the past (Phil 3:20; Heb 12: 22). This "something better" (v. 40) embraces the better hope, better promises, better covenant, better sacrifices, better and abiding possessions, and better resurrection which we now share as our heritage.

The "seeing" and "greeting" (v. 13) the promises of God is not insignificant. It is an expectation that changes our perspective in life and of our life. We see and greet them "from afar." This not only refers to time and distance but experience. We embrace these realities; we keep them in mind as we live our daily lives. Yet we do not live in a dreamland so focused on the future that we neglect the present. We need to learn the difference between the things which are important and that which is ultimate. That's our challenge. That's your challenge when God provides you a good job, but it's so good a job that it almost becomes your new religion. God provides you a nice place to live and your priority is more comfort at the expense of caring about others. God gives you a husband or wife and you are so in love that you neglect other relationships and begin to live in a little sweetheart bubble.

Notice how "not having received" and "having acknowledged" are contrasted. How do people "acknowledge" that they are strangers and exiles? By believing and acting on the promises of God, as Abraham did, even when there is nothing to indicate that they will be fulfilled in the near term. When we read that they died "not having received the promises" we understand this refers to the full realization. Hebrews 6:17 tells us that Abraham "obtained the promise" in the birth of Isaac and later his restoration when offered as a sacrifice (11:19). Verse 33 tells us that some "obtained promises." They did not receive the promise in the sense of its complete fulfillment in Christ and at his coming. F. F. Bruce explains that "they lived and died in prospect of a fulfillment which none of them experienced on earth; yet so real was that fulfillment to them that it gave them power to pass upstream, against the current of the environment, and to live on earth as citizens of that commonwealth whose foundations are firmly laid in the unseen and eternal order."[3]

In Christ and through the gospel we have another identity as strangers and exiles on earth. This life isn't all there is. Now, if you are not a child of God, then it's not surprising that your focus is only earthward. It's also not surprising that you invest so much time and energy in things that have some earthly importance and temporal satisfaction, but no eternal significance.

A PERSON WHOSE HEART DESIRES A BETTER COUNTRY (VV. 15–16)

How many of us desire a better country? Or do we really and secretly desire better and more fulfilling experiences here on earth? When we have an eternal perspective, it changes the way we live, the way we give, the way we spend our time; or it should. It determines how we decide to spend our Sunday morning, whether with God's people, in leisure activities, or doing projects around the house.

In speaking about a homeland, I'm the last person you will hear denigrating our country. I was born here. It was part of God's plan. I'm not always proud of my nation or its leadership but I'm not ashamed to be an American. I had a conversation recently with one of my doctors and told him, "I can't complain. I live in the greatest country in the world, and I'm headed toward an even better place." A doctor's time is precious so we didn't get too far, but there are times we can sow some seed to express the hope we have in Christ. Many have come to the United States, much like my ancestors or yours, to start a new life in what was called the New World. Many of you personally, for various reasons, have left your country of birth to settle in a foreign country. First-generation immigrants often have a difficult time adjusting to a new place even when they speak the

3. Bruce, *Hebrews*, 330.

same language. For those whose language is different there are additional challenges. For many the place they left is still their home where many of their loved ones still reside. They don't return home for many reasons—civil unrest, economic conditions, persecution. Some become American citizens, but they still feel like strangers. They may never lose their accent. Even their children who are born here and become American citizens at birth might be asked where they are from. I think that often changes in the generations that follow depending on whether language and traditions are passed on. Some ethnic groups do that more than others. Many become part of the great melting pot. Some live with a homesickness and nostalgia for the place they left. Others dream of visiting the land of their ancestors and learning about their history. Some people live with an identity crisis, not sure how they fit in, wondering if they would be better in another place. This is part of human experience. Yet, whatever our experience with our country of origin, whatever our relationship with our country of residence, whatever our political leanings, as believers first and foremost we are citizens of heaven and our allegiance is to Christ as head of his Church and Lord of the universe.

Being a pilgrim people, however, does not make us, in the words of an old expression, "too heavenly-minded to be of any earthly good." I'm not sure we can ever be too heavenly-minded, and if we are not of any earthly good the reason lies elsewhere. C. S. Lewis said, "If you read history you will find that the Christians who did most for the present world were just those who thought most of the next."[4] John Piper admits that theoretically it's possible to be so heavenly-minded that we are of no earthly good. He goes on to say, "I've never met one of those people. And I suspect, if I met one, the problem would not be that his mind is full of the glories of heaven, but that his mind is empty and his mouth is full of platitudes."[5] In the life of Abraham we see him as a man of action when the land was devasted by an invading army and Lot was captured. Abraham went with his men, defeated the enemy, and returned with those captured and all their possessions (Gen 14). Throughout the ages God's pilgrim people have been engaged in a world and in a land which was not their permanent dwelling place. We are not here as mere spectators. God has placed us where we are for his purposes, to live as his people and make him known.

4. Lewis, *Mere Christianity*, 134.

5. Piper, "I Do Not Aspire to Be a 'Regular Guy.'"

In Christ's coming as the Promised One, the promise was fulfilled which guarantees the fulfillment of all the promises of God (v. 40). Not one of his promises will fail. We will not experience their perfect and final fulfillment this side of eternity. But we can see them, welcome them, and acknowledge that we are destined to arrive at a better place in God's presence. We often hear the expression at funerals, "They are in a better place." We hear it used of people who never had any place or time for God in their lives, who never gave any indication of a relationship with Jesus Christ. It's often said to provide comfort and make people feel better about someone's death. It's a false comfort when used for someone who was not united to Christ by faith in his sacrifice for sins. That someone is in a "better place" is true only for the children of God. As believers we should be able to have a biblical perspective on living and dying.

I found this quote in an epistle written to Diognetus in the second or third century AD:

> For the Christians are distinguished from other men neither by country, nor language, nor the customs which they observe . . . They dwell in their own countries, but simply as sojourners. As citizens, they share in all things with others, and yet endure all things as if foreigners. Every foreign land is to them as their native country, and every land of their birth as a land of strangers . . . They pass their days on earth, but they are citizens of heaven.[6]

Can that be said of us today?

A PERSON OF WHOM GOD IS NOT ASHAMED (V. 16)

Several times in Scripture we find the expression, "God of Abraham, the God of Isaac, and the God of Jacob" (Exod 3:6; Matt 22:32). So firm was their commitment to their heavenly calling that God was not ashamed of them. We must at least ask ourselves the question at times, "Is God ashamed of me?" In other words, am I living in such a way that God could not say this about me? I'm sure there have been times in all of our lives when our actions and decisions have not pleased God and we experienced failure. None of these believers were perfect in their obedience. And as I said earlier, God does not bring up their failures in this passage. But the orientation of their hearts and the direction of their lives was to please him by faithful obedience.

6. Early Church Texts, "Epistle to Diognetus - chapters 5–7."

Think about this for a moment: a city prepared by God for his people. Over the past year we've seen people flee the cities. It's not the first time. People flee. Others arrive. Many feel like they are stuck in the city because of family or work, or because they can't afford to leave the city. But God is preparing a city with such incredible beauty and satisfying glory, beyond your imagination. Whatever you can imagine how that city will look, it's more glorious, it's far better. As a matter of fact, we can imagine so little by our senses. But we see it, we welcome it, we grasp it by faith, faith in a God of promise, who keeps his promises, a God who is unchangeable, unshakeable, unstoppable, seated on his throne, and worthy of everything we have to offer him. Of course, what makes this city most glorious is the presence of our Savior! As a matter of fact, the most important thing about the city is that the God we worship is there, the One we will worship for all the endless ages of eternity.

Let us think about this in some practical ways. Do you have excuses Sunday morning for missing corporate worship? If you are not careful, other people will plan your Sundays with events and invitations that on any other day might be welcome. But Sunday? Your commitment to the local church should be the excuse (reason) why you don't accept invitations or plans made for you by others. Establish that priority and most people will stop asking you to commit to their plans. If ever your church attendance becomes (or is) an inconvenience, if your giving goes mostly in one direction (to you), if your Bible sits unopened day after day in your home, if you are too busy to stop to pray in dependence upon God and in intercession for others, if you are too unconcerned about telling people about Jesus, you can be certain of this—you have lost what it means to be a stranger in exile! You are tied so closely to your own pursuits that heaven seems like a foreign land. You love this life you have made for yourself so much that heaven holds little place in your heart and mind. What kind of person are you or seeking to be? Are you so settled here on earth, so satisfied with your earthly life and accomplishments, that the heavenly country is far from your mind?

Are you seeking a homeland? Or are you so comfortable and content today in this world that its attractions have captured you, body and soul? Christ and the gospel call us to live in this world as strangers and exiles, not clinging too tightly to our earthly possessions and ambitions, enjoying his good graces toward us when we prosper and enjoy good health, ever mindful that whether we live or die we are the Lord's (Rom 14:8), and that our departure from this world is not a question of if, but of when and how (Heb 9:27). These truths should not cause us to be morbid or overly reflective about death. We don't go around wringing our hands in despair. You are here today by God's grace. Your next breath is a gift. Tomorrow you might be in eternity. We live today with joy and purpose, joy in our sins forgiven and the promise of eternal life, purpose in serving God and others for whatever time he allots us.

2

Great Joy of the Gospel

Luke 2:1–20

1 In those days a decree went out from Caesar Augustus that all the
world should be registered. 2 This was the first registration when
Quirinius was governor of Syria. 3 And all went to be registered,
each to his own town. 4 And Joseph also went up from Galilee,
from the town of Nazareth, to Judea, to the city of David, which
is called Bethlehem, because he was of the house and lineage of
David, 5 to be registered with Mary, his betrothed, who was with
child. 6 And while they were there, the time came for her to give
birth. 7 And she gave birth to her firstborn son and wrapped him
in swaddling cloths and laid him in a manger, because there was
no place for them in the inn. 8 And in the same region there were
shepherds out in the field, keeping watch over their flock by night.
9 And an angel of the Lord appeared to them, and the glory of
the Lord shone around them, and they were filled with great fear.
10 And the angel said to them, "Fear not, for behold, I bring you
good news of great joy that will be for all the people. 11 For unto
you is born this day in the city of David a Savior, who is Christ
the Lord. 12 And this will be a sign for you: you will find a baby
wrapped in swaddling cloths and lying in a manger." 13 And suddenly there was with the angel a multitude of the heavenly host
praising God and saying, 14 "Glory to God in the highest, and on
earth peace among those with whom he is pleased!" 15 When the
angels went away from them into heaven, the shepherds said to
one another, "Let us go over to Bethlehem and see this thing that
has happened, which the Lord has made known to us." 16 And

> they went with haste and found Mary and Joseph, and the baby
> lying in a manger. 17 And when they saw it, they made known the
> saying that had been told them concerning this child. 18 And all
> who heard it wondered at what the shepherds told them. 19 But
> Mary treasured up all these things, pondering them in her heart.
> 20 And the shepherds returned, glorifying and praising God for all
> they had heard and seen, as it had been told them.

THE PASSAGE BEFORE US is one that my family has read for years on Christmas morning. Lord willing, we will read it again this year and years to come. It is a story that has become so familiar that we wonder if there is anything new to discover. Yet, we don't need to discover anything new. We just need to discover anew the One to whom this passage testifies, a discovery which never ends. And when we leave the scene we should be filled with wonder and follow the shepherds in praise. Many Americans bemoan today what has been called the "War on Christmas." I sympathize with many of their concerns, yet I have a greater concern. The greatest concern is not that the city of Philadelphia wanted to change "Christmas Village" to "Holiday Village" a few years ago and backtracked after the protests of citizens (of which I was one and wrote a protest letter). Even more concerning to believers should be how little the entrance of the Christ into the world receives notice throughout the year. Yes, Jesus is the reason for the season. More than that, he is the Prince of Peace, King of Kings to whom all owe homage, and he will not be content with lip service one season of the year. Jesus is not seasonal, available Christmas and Easter, like the seasonal aisles in the supermarket. If your Jesus is a seasonal one and shows up once or twice a year, then you have not yet met the real Jesus of which Luke speaks.

Verses 1–7 place Jesus in perspective of world history and family activity. There are few details about the Savior's birth, but the ones given are unusual—swaddling cloths and a manger. Some have found an allusion to the tomb with mention of the swaddling cloths (v. 7) and the linen cloth in which the body of Jesus was wrapped after his death (23:53). There is more space devoted to the census than to the actual birth. The census, probably for tax purposes, is mentioned four times (2:1, 2, 3, 5) and was a reminder of the alien rule of Rome and the demand of loyalty to an emperor which compromised loyalty to the Lord. Verses 8–20 give us a divine perspective as the angel appears to the shepherds announcing the Savior's birth and who is then joined by the hosts of heaven in offering praise. The heart of the passage is found in the proclamation of the birth of royalty and the good news of great joy. The good news is not only in an event but in the arrival of a person, in the Savior, the Messiah promised by the prophets. This is good news of great joy which we need to experience throughout the year.

GREAT JOY OF THE GOSPEL IS INSEPARABLE FROM THE HISTORICAL AND MIRACULOUS BIRTH OF THE DAVIDIC KING

Luke sets the birth of Jesus anchored solidly in history in the Roman Empire of the first century. Caesar Augustus was the grandnephew of Julius Caesar. During the Christmas season we witness a relatively new phenomena called billboard battles—"You know it's a myth. This season celebrate reason." Or, "You know it's real. This season celebrate Jesus." Of course, many want it to be a myth. A myth has no real authority, makes no demands, changes no lives, and does not warn of the consequences of rejection. It has been said that atheists have their own holiday, April Fool's Day (Ps 14:1), but I sense more pity than disdain for atheists. We have nothing to fear from atheism. They have everything to fear, which will not be squelched by the loud protests, as if saying, "I don't believe that God exists" or "I know there is no God" will make it so.

The words "In those days" (v. 1) begin a solemn recounting of the events which led to Christ's birth in the obscure village of Bethlehem, not far removed geographically from Jerusalem but a world away from the center of power and influence. There is a narrowing focus in the text from Augustus to Quirinius to Joseph and then to Jesus; from Rome to Syria to Nazareth in Galilee, Bethlehem in Judea, to the countryside. "Going up" and "city of David" (v. 4) invite the reader to expect Jerusalem. Luke upsets these expectations in telling us that Bethlehem would be the place of royal birth in fulfillment of Micah 5:2. The "firstborn" possessed the right of inheritance. Jesus received the birthright through Joseph, who was from the "house and family of David."

The simplicity of this story has become so familiar that over the years we have witnessed the addition of details to satisfy our curiosity to know more than the Bible tells us. Who hasn't read the Christmas story or seen nativity films which picture Mary and Joseph arriving haggard from their long voyage of about ninety miles from Nazareth to Bethlehem on the very night of Jesus' birth only to encounter an innkeeper who shoos them away because his hotel is filled with paying travelers. The innkeeper shouts, "No room," and slams the shutters closed. Many of the additions are innocent or legendary but there is no reason to believe that the family of Jesus arrived at the last minute because they didn't plan well or make sufficient plans for lodging ahead of time. There is no indication that there was a commercial inn in Bethlehem with a grumpy innkeeper who didn't know who he was sending away to find lodging in a stable.

From what we know of life in that time it would not be surprising that Mary and Joseph had arrived several days before the birth of Christ and had found lodging with relatives, friends, or in a public shelter used by travelers. The word "inn" has the idea of "guestroom" in Luke 22:11; translated "guestroom" it refers to the upper room of the Passover meal. In those times houses often were built with animals living in an area under or near the living quarters. Whether they were in a public guesthouse or a guestroom, it is not surprising that there was not sufficient space or privacy for a pregnant woman to give birth or that the family would seek a place for the birth of the baby away from the eyes of other travelers. Although a virgin birth, there is no mention of a painless birth. What is certainly true and of importance is the lowly place of Christ's birth, in a stable, cave, or guestroom, and laid in a feeding trough as a bed. Some have suggested the stable was a cave. In Bethlehem a basilica, the Church of the Nativity, was built by Constantine in the fourth century over a cave site, the traditional site of the birth of Christ. The Christmas lullaby "Away in a Manger" surely exaggerates a bit when we sing, "The little Lord Jesus no crying he makes." Yet we can never exaggerate the importance of Christ's birth anchored in history, a humble birth for the Messianic king.

GREAT JOY OF THE GOSPEL IS HIDDEN FROM THE MIGHTY AND REVEALED ONLY TO THE LOWLY

The story moves from a context of neighbors/relatives to worldwide overtones. "All the world" (v. 1) asserts Caesar's sovereignty, but now there is a rival king and there comes a question of allegiance. Joseph obeys the imperial decree, yet the birth will not be made known to kings and governors but to shepherds as God bypasses the rich and powerful. Many have wanted to know more about the early childhood and adolescence of Jesus. Matthew and Luke tell us a little about the circumstances of Jesus' birth, and Luke has one story about his going to the temple in Jerusalem when he was twelve.

Jesus' birth to a virgin named Mary signifies that Jesus is present as the miraculous gift of a gracious God, the God-given goal of all human history. If you want to know about Jesus, if you want to really know him, you have to meet him as King. You have to bow before him. And if in the pride of your heart you stand in your own goodness or your religion or your morality you cannot be forgiven until you say, "Come reign in my life, O King Jesus!" What the Gospels consider most important about Jesus is not his family or his youth but rather his identification as Savior, Messiah, and Lord. He is the Deliverer, the Anointed One, and the Absolute Sovereign. Luke does not explain these titles but their meaning will become more evident in time.

The census of Augustus provides the backdrop and the impetus for Joseph and Mary to leave Nazareth and travel to Bethlehem. God uses the decree of a human emperor and turns it for his own purposes. The one who orders the census so that "all the world" would be taxed—the extent of the Roman Empire and for purposes of temporal benefit—had no idea that in the movement of people back to their ancestral homes God would accomplish something of universal and everlasting significance. The city of David would naturally have been seen as a reference to Jerusalem. David was born in Bethlehem but Jerusalem became the capital of the united kingdom of Israel after the death of Saul. God signifies by this that the royal birthright of Jesus Christ was not dependent on governing from or identifying with the geographical space occupied by the kings of Israel. All this detail demonstrates that God bypasses the rich and powerful and reveals himself to the poor and lowly. It is not that those who are rich and powerful cannot be saved. But they cannot be saved without seeing their spiritual poverty and weakness. As long as anyone trusts in their position, their wealth, their privileges, or their accomplishments, there is no hope for salvation as presented in Luke 1:52: "He has brought down the mighty from their thrones and exalted those of humble estate."

At this moment in history, Julius Caesar was regarded as divinity. His grandnephew and adopted son Augustus was called the "son of God" and "savior" and anticipated deification upon his death. He was reigning during a time of relative peace enforced by the Roman armies. His rival brought real peace in inaugurating a competing kingdom that one day would be established forever. The offer of peace through the Christ indicated the deficiency of Roman peace. Zachariah had prophesied that Israel would be "delivered from the hand of [their] enemies" (1:74). The "glory of the Lord" (2:9), God's majestic presence, was connected historically with the tabernacle and temple. Now that glory is manifested in the countryside apart from religious edifices, which signified that worship would be detached from holy places. The "good news" announced here becomes more and more qualified in Luke's Gospel and its recipients. Consider 4:16, "The Spirit of the Lord is upon me, because he has anointed me to proclaim good news to the poor," and 7:22, "Go and tell John what you have seen and heard . . . the poor have good news preached to them."

GREAT JOY OF THE GOSPEL REMOVES FEAR AND PROVIDES GENUINE PEACE AND UNCONTAINABLE PRAISE

The emperor Augustus exercised his temporal and limited authority to move people from the places where they lived to the places where they had been born. The God of the universe exercises his unbounded and universal authority and moves people from darkness into light, from sadness and despair to joy. This great joy becomes a settled disposition of hearts which have found that which truly satisfies, which brings lasting contentment. It is that condition that can only be known through forgiveness of sins, hence the emphasis on a Savior, on a Deliverer, on the defeat of God's enemies, and on a kingdom ruled by the Son of God. Joy cannot be understood apart from Christ's sacrifice for sin, who for the joy that was set before him endured the cross (Heb 12:2). "There was no outward glory, no angel choir, no triumphant display. Yet that cross was the ultimate revelation of the power and wisdom of God."[1]

We should not be surprised that the shepherds were filled with fear, as were Zachariah and Mary (1:12, 29) and later the disciples at the transfiguration (9:34). We would all be terrified and unsettled in an encounter with the Almighty. The angel calms the shepherds' fear. God's grace shows his desire to be known. This gospel joy is the greatest joy. It has nothing to do with what we do or how hard we work at having or maintaining it. It is given to us and we do nothing for it. We receive it through the gospel; it takes up residence in our lives and at times gets lost in the clutter of our daily existence. Verse 14 provides a rare and awesome glimpse into heavenly praise as God's entourage, this heavenly host, addresses earth about Christ's coming. "Glory to God in the highest, and on earth peace among those with whom

1. Rhodes, *Man of Sorrows*, 67.

he is pleased!" This peace is a harmonious relationship which can exist between God and humans. The heavens rejoice at what God is undertaking in bringing salvation. People on earth, on whom God has shown his favor and grace, experience peace and the benefits of Christ's coming.

As Christians, regardless of what takes place in the world, we are not sitting by gloomily, waiting for Jesus to return to accomplish his purposes. He has already set in motion the fulfillment of his purposes, and we await the consummation. We share in that event as the shepherds did "who made known" (v. 17) what had been told them about the child. What had they been told? What did they make known? That a Savior is born! Many Christians are waiting for Jesus to come again to do his work. He is coming again and will accomplish his purposes. He is also now doing his work and does his work in some measure through those who have seen and heard the great things of God. Sometimes what he is doing may be as little perceived as was his birth in an obscure town away from palaces and the places of power and prestige. It may be in the ghettoes of our country and in nations around the world where the gospel has penetrated more deeply than we see it here in our own nation. But make no mistake, the new age has dawned. For those who have been snatched from darkness, who have seen this great light, there is cause for praise and delight in following the shepherds in making known what has been told them about the child. Deliverance and praise always lead to witness. How can we be silent, those of us who have heard and received this good news and know the great joy of the gospel?

So what do we conclude from this passage where we see God at work, the heavens speak, the shepherds amazed, prophecies fulfilled, and Mary reflecting? How do we respond to the arrival of salvation into the world? We understand several truths:

1. God's higher purposes are at work through the decree of an earthly emperor. Let kings and presidents do what they will. God will do what only he can do. There is much to lament in our nation today. Yet there is no reason for despair. God turns the acts and commands of dictators to further his will.
2. When he says, "Fear not!" your fears need to cease in the peace and joy of good news deliverance.
3. Heaven and earth give praise to this child. We either join in praise out of grateful hearts or lead empty lives of complaint and ingratitude,

fearful and joyless, celebrating a holiday or season, ignoring or indifferent to the Savior, the King.

4. In Bethlehem, a little town, a baby had a humble birth, but God made this event one of the greatest in all history, an event that is ignored at one's own peril. Will you live today as did the shepherds in verse 20, glorifying and praising God?

In a quote attributed to a sermon by James Francis which came to be known as "One Solitary Life," it was written that all the armies that ever marched, and all the navies that ever sailed, and all the parliaments that ever sat, and all the kings that ever reigned, put together have not affected the life of man upon this earth as powerfully as this One Solitary Life. A new king has been enthroned. "Whether we recognize his rule or not, the Bible is crystal clear that Jesus is now sovereign over all creation."[2] Is he your Savior, your King?

2. Rhodes, *Man of Sorrows*, 140.

3

Radical Discipleship

Mark 1:16–20

> 16 Passing alongside the Sea of Galilee, he saw Simon and Andrew the brother of Simon casting a net into the sea, for they were fishermen. 17 And Jesus said to them, "Follow me, and I will make you become fishers of men." 18 And immediately they left their nets and followed him. 19 And going on a little farther, he saw James the son of Zebedee and John his brother, who were in their boat mending the nets. 20 And immediately he called them, and they left their father Zebedee in the boat with the hired servants and followed him.

WE SEE IN THE background to this event that Isaiah spoke, John the Baptist spoke, God the Father spoke, and the Holy Spirit appeared. Satan and angels also appear in the preparation of the announcement when Jesus speaks for the first time in Mark's Gospel and announces the nearness of the kingdom. We see that Mark is short on details. He gives us the big picture in identifying all the characters involved in this drama, the drama of redemption. Jesus is unlike all other kings. In Deuteronomy 17 Moses instructed Israel concerning the king that they would one day appoint. He gave three negative stipulations: he must not acquire many horses (v. 16); he must not acquire many wives (v. 17a); he must not acquire excessive silver and gold (v. 17b). In 2 Samuel 7:12–17, God promised King David a son who would be king forever. Notice what the Bible says about Solomon in 1 Kings 10:21:

"All King Solomon's drinking vessels were of gold, and all the vessels of the House of the Forest of Lebanon were of pure gold." In verse 26, "Solomon gathered together chariots and horsemen. He had 1,400 chariots and 12,000 horsemen." In chapter 11:3, "he had 700 wives, princesses, and 300 concubines." In other words, he had excessive gold, excessive horses, and excessive wives. Solomon is not the ultimate Son/King who was promised in 2 Samuel 7. Another son of David would come. This king would be rich, and "yet for [our] sake he became poor, so that [we] by his poverty might become rich" (2 Cor 8:9). This king would not own horses. He would have to borrow a donkey to ride into Jerusalem (John 12:14). This king would not have many wives. He would have one bride and he would give his own life for her (Eph 5:25–27).

After the announcement of the kingdom we might expect something of cosmic importance, some great undertaking to further the king's agenda—setting up a throne or collecting tribute or taxes. What we find is different. We find Jesus by the sea with common laborers. I don't mean that in a demeaning sense. But Jesus did not begin his public ministry in Jerusalem, a place of influence and power, among the political and religious leaders. In Acts the apostles are called "unlearned and ignorant men" (Acts 4:13) in the eyes of the elite of society. He is calling fishermen to his mission as laborers in his kingdom. The inauguration of the kingdom of God does not come with cosmic outward displays of power, although local miracles of Jesus gave evidence of the king's arrival. With the calling of socially insignificant people in an unnoticed corner of a Roman province, Jesus launched a movement of ultimately huge dimensions which at its beginning was barely noticed on the world stage. We are reminded that God has a different value scale than we do.

From now on Jesus will be accompanied by his disciples, twelve men and only twelve, although there were other companions along the way. He knew that he could better pour his life into a small group of men and prepare them to carry on his mission after his departure. They will sometimes fail and disappoint him. One of them will betray him and show that he was never a genuine believer even after three years of personal contact with Jesus. But these men are crucial for the accomplishment of his mission. Although flawed people, something has taken place in their lives which completely reorients them. They follow Jesus promptly and completely. You don't get to come to Jesus on your own terms then go your own merry way.

That's not an option. Jesus here takes the initiative. You may have thought you were seeking him but only because he first sought you.

I find it interesting that Mark doesn't give his readers any background to this call. We know from John's Gospel that these men had been introduced to Jesus a year earlier. The material in Luke's Gospel is arranged so that the call to be "fishers of men" followed the casting out of demons, the healing of Simon's mother-in-law, and the fishing miracle where Jesus caused the nets to become so full that both of their boats overflowed with fish. From Mark's point of view, even though there may be more background to the call, he wants to focus on the call itself and the nature of the response. This call is radical and the response is radical. He wants his readers to consider the radical nature of Jesus' call and the radical response of the disciples. It's radical in many ways, not the least because of the authority and the claims of the one who issues the call and the immediate and surprising response of the ones called.

FOLLOW ME—A CALL TO A SPECIAL RELATIONSHIP WITH JESUS

Are you a follower of Jesus Christ? Is your following conditional or unconditional? What comes to mind when you think of a disciple? Of course you think of the Twelve whom Jesus called. You might also think of others throughout history—missionaries, evangelists, pastors—whom God used in extraordinary ways, people who have sacrificed their fortunes, left their families, or died in faraway places. The language here is not used simply to describe what one must do to become a member of the Twelve but rather what any person must do to become a follower of Jesus. From now on they would not serve their own interests and desires but those of Jesus who called them. They did not know everything that would take place on the journey. Neither do we. They knew the destination, the eventual full establishment of the kingdom which had arrived in a mystery form hidden from eyes which have not been opened.

In this text today we have men who left their businesses in order to follow Jesus Christ. Normally disciples chose who they would follow. Jesus reverses that practice. This presents a challenge for us. Does God expect me to respond to Jesus in any way similar to their response? How can the millions of people whom we consider to be ordinary Christians follow Jesus? They are businessmen, students, housewives, retirees, and construction workers. Are they following Jesus? Have they responded to his call? Many Christians feel they are not really following Christ unless they are in what's often called full-time ministry. Is that true? Of course not.

Two words or phrases might help us here. We live in the "already / not yet." We are already redeemed by the blood of Christ with forgiveness of all our sins (Col 1:13–14), not yet completely free from sin and temptation (1 John 1:8; Rom 8:23). We have already received the Spirit of adoption (Rom 8:16), but have not entered into the full possession of our inheritance of the glory yet to be revealed (Rom 8:18). We are already saved by grace (Rom 8:24; Eph 2:8), but not yet fully delivered until salvation is completed at the redemption of the body at the resurrection (Rom 8:23). We are already sanctified (1 Cor 1:2), and God continues his work of sanctifying us (1 Thess 5:23). We are already seated "in the heavenly realms" (Eph 2:6), yet living with the promise that Jesus is preparing our future place (John 14:2). The kingdom of God has been inaugurated (Mark 1:14–15), but the kingdoms of this world remain in rebellion until Christ comes again (Rev 11:15). All these blessings and promises are found in Christ and "we cannot think of, or enjoy, the blessings of the gospel either isolated from each other or separated from the Benefactor himself."[1] We have so much already in Christ, but when we look at the world, at crime, violence, child prostitution, human trafficking, drug cartels, and dictators, we see that Christ's kingdom has "not yet" fully come. So we pray—your will be done on earth as it is in heaven (Matt 6:10).

To follow Jesus there is a call. To follow Jesus there is cost. To follow Jesus there is a cross. It's far more than the Four Spiritual Laws, where God loves you and offers a wonderful plan for your life. There's truth to that but it's easy to read our plan into his plan. A call-less Christianity, a cross-less Christianity, a cost-less Christianity, is a Christ-less Christianity. This is not about volunteerism. There is no room for negotiation. There is no give-and-take. There is no "first let me" (Luke 9:61) do something or other. Following Jesus, saying no to yourself, your plans, and yes to God, does not diminish you, it does not enslave you. It frees you to live life according to God's plan. God does not save you to fulfill your life but to "fill full" your life. Fillfullment, not fulfillment. Certainly you will be misunderstood at times when you answer this call. But you will be investing your life for things of eternal value.

1. Ferguson, *Holy Spirit*, 102.

I WILL MAKE YOU FISHERS OF MEN— ON MISSION WITH JESUS

Here is his promise. He will make you become something you are not, something you cannot be without him. We recognize that we have in Jesus' words a mixed metaphor. Those whom Jesus calls to be fishers of men are called to rescue others so they can live. They are rescued from impending judgment in light of the intrusion of the kingdom of God into this world. The call and promise remain the same; the way of response differs from person to person and culture to culture. What remains the same is this—the call is a radical call to ministry that demands a radical response. Jesus will never leave you, but he will never leave you the same!

Would this be a legitimate question in light of Jesus' words: If I am not becoming a fisher of men, what needs to change so that I may follow Jesus? I can't answer that for you. It's not simply a question of learning more. There are Christians who know the Bible inside and out yet do very little for the kingdom. They have a very privatized and individual salvation that is more about their rescue from judgment than about rescuing others. Ask yourself, "Am I involved in people's lives in some way to bring them out of the waters of judgment into the kingdom?" We're not talking about how many you've won to Christ. We're not counting noses. We're not giving prizes for being a great soulwinner. But are you praying for lost people, sowing seeds of the word of God in their lives, and seeking to make the most of opportunities God has given you?

THEY LEFT THEIR NETS / THEIR FATHER— TOTAL COMMITMENT TO HIS CAUSE

It's one thing to leave your trade, but your father? Not even the closest, most obligatory family tie can keep the brothers there, so powerful is Jesus' call. What do you think of the actions of these men? Andrew and Simon Peter, James and John leave their businesses to follow Jesus Christ. This is the life they have known. They have an investment in equipment. At least for James and John, this is a family business and a fairly successful one, including other hired workers. We recognize that this is a radical and costly action. Right away we recognize, however, some difference with our situation today. There is no way that we can physically follow Jesus in the twenty-first century. He is not here! If I quit my job today, where is Jesus that I could follow him?

Does this then make this command irrelevant to modern-day Christians? Or are we still called to follow him, only in a non-geographic way?

You might ask yourself, "Is Jesus calling me to respond like these four men did? Should I leave the means of supporting my family and providing for living in this world? Must I leave my occupation and my family in this way?" Not in this way, but in some way! Most people are not ready or called to do what they did! If we were in Andrew and Simon's places, would we have responded similarly? That is, if our circumstances were identical would our response also be? I tend to think that the answer for many is yes. If Jesus Christ walked into your workplace tomorrow morning and said, "Follow me and I will make you fishers of men," I believe you would leave your desk or your classroom and follow him.

Why do we struggle with this radical call and radical response? Why do we not sense an emergency, an urgency to do so? We can't really see the urgency of this call apart from the gospel. The gospel of Jesus Christ is the basis of this radical call and radical response. The cross of Jesus Christ declares an emergency requiring decisive action. The gospel is a message to be presented, not merely a canned presentation for religious change. Witnessing happens naturally when coupled with radical life change. Jesus has just announced the arrival of the kingdom of God. He declares that this is the beginning of the end of the world and world powers when God will bring judgment and salvation. Then he issues this radical call—repent, believe the good news, follow me. He has come to die for sinners so they can be rescued from the great judgment of God and so that rescued sinners can join him in his mission. In a real and profound sense anyone who follows Jesus gives up a normal life. For many the question is not "Should I follow Jesus?" but "How do I follow Jesus?" Has my life been fundamentally reordered as a result of a radical response to his call? We can follow others as they follow Christ. But if you follow men you will be disappointed at times. Jesus never fails!

In 1904 William Borden graduated from a Chicago high school. As heir to the Borden family fortune, he was already wealthy. For his high school graduation present, his parents gave sixteen-year-old William a trip around the world. As the young man traveled throughout Asia, the Middle East, and Europe, he felt a growing burden for the world's hurting people. Finally, Borden wrote home about his desire to be a missionary. One friend expressed disbelief that Borden was throwing his life away as a missionary. In response, Borden wrote two words in the back of his Bible: "No reserves." During his college years at Yale University, Borden made an entry in his personal journal that defined what his classmates were seeing in him. That entry said simply: "Say 'no' to self and 'yes' to Jesus every time." Upon graduation from Yale, Borden turned down some high-paying job offers. In his Bible, he wrote two more words: "No retreats."

Borden went on to do graduate work at Princeton Seminary in New Jersey. When he finished his studies at Princeton, he sailed for China. Because he was hoping to work with Muslims, he stopped first in Egypt to study Arabic. While there, he contracted spinal meningitis. Within a month, twenty-five-year-old William Borden was dead. Was Borden's untimely death a waste? Not in God's perspective. Prior to his death, Borden had written two more words in his Bible. Underneath the words "No reserves" and "No retreats," he had written: "No regrets." God used his testimony to raise up many who surrendered to world missions.

Your circumstances might be drastically different from William Borden's. Yet your Savior is the same, the mission is the same, the urgency is the same, the spirit of sacrifice and commitment is the same. But we cannot remain the same! There's a call, there's a cost, and there's a cross. It may be stepping into some unknown territory, but as long as you follow Jesus you will be on the right path. Follow Jesus and he will make you become a fisher of men.

4

The Gospel and Religion

Acts 17:30–31

> 30 The times of ignorance God overlooked, but now he commands
> all people everywhere to repent, 31 because he has fixed a day on
> which he will judge the world in righteousness by a man whom he
> has appointed; and of this he has given assurance to all by raising
> him from the dead.

ACTS 17 PRESENTS THE apostle Paul's foray into enemy territory on his second missionary journey. These were not his personal enemies to be treated with disdain and hatred, but a gospel confrontation with false religion and religionists who in spite of their sincere efforts remained separated from God in their ignorance and spiritual blindness. He had been chased from Thessalonica after his preaching caused a riot. He was followed by his persecutors to Berea where he found a great opening for the gospel and people eager to study the Scriptures. Now he arrives at Athens. Through his experience there we are challenged to ask ourselves how we obey God in making Christ known through the gospel in a society which values and validates much that is in opposition to the word of God.

A few years ago at one of our leadership team meetings we discussed the concept of contextualization. You don't need to retain the big word. It's simply giving God's answers to the questions people are asking or should be asking (giving answers which they may not want) and in ways that can be understood. It's meeting people where they are, finding that point of contact or starting point in our gospel witness. In other words, how do we faithfully communicate the gospel of Jesus Christ in a world and society that by turns is ignorant of, indifferent to, or hostile towards the exclusive claims of Jesus Christ as Savior, Lord, and Coming King?

In the film and book *Life of Pi*, Pi is first a Hindu, then a Christian, then a Muslim, then all at the same time. He just wants to love God. He tries to understand God through the lens of each religion and comes to recognize benefits in each one. Eventually, his family decides to leave their zoo over a land dispute with the government and sells the animals to various zoos around the world before emigrating to Canada. In the second part of the novel, Pi's family embarks on a Japanese freighter to Canada carrying some of the animals from their zoo, but a few days out of port, the ship meets a storm and sinks, resulting in his family's death. During the storm, Pi escapes death in a small lifeboat with a spotted hyena, an injured zebra, and an orangutan. As Pi strives to survive among the animals, much to Pi's distress the hyena kills the zebra, then the orangutan. At this point, it is discovered that a Bengal tiger named Richard Parker had been hiding under the boat's tarpaulin; it kills and eats the hyena. Frightened, Pi constructs a small raft out of flotation devices, tethers it to the boat, and retreats to it. He delivers some of the fish and water he harvests to Richard Parker to keep him satisfied, conditioning Richard Parker not to threaten him by rocking the boat and causing seasickness while blowing a whistle. Eventually, Richard Parker learns to tolerate Pi's presence and they both live in the boat. Pi recounts various events while adrift, including discovering an island of carnivorous algae inhabited by meerkats. After 227 days, the lifeboat washes up onto the coast of Mexico and Richard Parker immediately escapes into the nearby jungle.

In the third part of the novel, two officials from the Japanese Ministry of Transport speak to Pi to ascertain why the ship sank. When they do not believe his story, he tells an alternative story of human brutality, in which Pi was adrift on a lifeboat with his mother, a sailor with a broken leg, and the ship's cook, who killed the sailor and Pi's mother and cut them up to use as bait and food. Parallels to Pi's first story lead the Japanese officials to believe that the orangutan represents his mother, the zebra represents the sailor, the hyena represents the cook, and Richard Parker is Pi himself. After giving all the relevant information, Pi asks which of the two stories they prefer. Since the officials cannot prove which story is true and neither is relevant to the reasons behind the shipwreck, they choose the story with the animals.

Pi thanks them and says, "and so it goes with God." Many live their lives with a feeling that there is a God or have an emotional attachment to the idea of God. The facts are either unimportant or unverifiable. Like many of our contemporaries, what is important is to believe something. And so it was with the Athenians.

The city of Athens was a center of Greek culture and intellectual pursuits. Although it was but a shadow of its former glory in the "golden age" of the fourth and fifth century BC, Athens remained an important city and was badly in need of the light of the gospel. This encounter provides a prime example of Paul's ministry among the Gentiles followed by eighteen months in Corinth, a city which eclipsed Athens and was now the leading city of that region of the world. This stopover in Athens is part of the advance of the gospel throughout Europe and provides an example to us as Christians in the twenty-first century in answering the question, How do we advance gospel truth claims against competing truth claims in our day?

THERE MUST BE PATIENT PERSUASION WITH THE TRUTH OF THE GOSPEL

We see Paul in Athens speaking first in the synagogue then in the marketplace. We see that his spirit was "provoked" (v. 16) by the idolatry which led him to patiently reason every day with people in the synagogue and in the marketplace (v. 17). When we speak of patience we are not talking about praying for years about how to approach someone with the gospel and waiting for some kind of special urgency before we open our mouths and speak. Of course we pray, and we may pray for years before someone comes to Christ. But our praying must never become a substitute for speaking. We never know how much time a person has. We never know if there will be another opportunity. We should be gripped with some kind of divine urgency.

Of course, you may be misrepresented and mocked: Paul was called a "babbler" (v. 18). Some have seen here the image of a bird pecking seeds or someone who picked up scraps of ideas here and there. Some have conjectured that Paul preached about Jesus' parable of the sower. Paul was accused of preaching about "foreign deities" (v. 18). You may also be misunderstood at times and need to clarify the message. As in all witnessing you need to find a place to begin. Paul observed that the audience was "very religious" (v. 22). There's some ambiguity in the word "religious" but these people were devout. There are things we can commend in people who are not believers. It is not a blanket endorsement of their religion or their non-religion. Paul found points of contact and spoke of altars and temples (vv. 23–24). Paul could've called them pagans and idolaters, which they were. We may accommodate our speech, but we dare not accommodate the truth to make it more palatable. Paul wants to teach people that God is knowable. The audience was open to receiving instruction about an unknown god that they cannot worship unless they know him. Paul spoke of an impersonal "what" they worshiped (v. 23) and introduced them to a personal God "who made world" (v. 24).

THERE MUST BE A PROFOUND DEPENDENCE ON THE SPIRIT OF GOD

You may often stand alone in the midst of brilliant people who question or mock your views. You are competing in the marketplace of ideas, and when you are faithful to the gospel you do not really stand alone. Paul understood his audience. Among them were Epicureans and Stoics. Many people fall on one side or the other of Epicureanism or Stoicism. The Epicureans were thoroughgoing materialists. For them there was no life beyond this one. They were indifferent to whether gods existed, without completely denying the possibility. The Stoics believed in divine providence to the point of pantheism and that there was some kind of divine spark in all humanity.

We never know what will take place in our gospel encounters with people. There is often a sense of exhaustion, a sense of fatigue, a sense of disappointment when we see people who we have poured our lives into walk away from the gospel and the church. Or we see ministries that we've been pouring our lives into with little evident growth, and we feel as though we are failing because we don't have the right stuff to have successful ministry. Scripture calls us to faithfulness, and Scripture tells us that the fruit that Jesus brings forward often happens long after we have eyes to see those things. I want to encourage you that as you commit to faithfulness in the service that's been entrusted to you, don't attempt ministry by your own abilities and by your own gifts. And don't despair when you look around and say, "I don't see what I expected to see."

THERE MUST BE A POWERFUL PROCLAMATION OF REPENTANCE AND THE JUDGMENT OF GOD

We don't have a different message for intellectuals and for others, the elite or the common person. Paul was not content to remain in the synagogue where there might be a better reception. Paul used the Athenians' language, quoted their poets, and sought to reach them in terms they understood, but he never compromised the gospel. His message was rooted in Old Testament thought. Paul could quote their poets without sanctioning their entire belief systems. Paul does not hold back from confronting and correcting. He speaks of a God who has been neglected and offended. He announces a personal God, a Creator and Judge, and declares that all people are of common descent (v. 26). He will then call upon his listeners to repent.

The world (coworkers, family, neighbors) won't mind your doing good things—feeding the poor, caring for the homeless, projects to alleviate human suffering, building projects, or working to stop sex trafficking. These are good things in which we may be engaged as God leads. The problem comes when we are not engaged in calling people to what God has called them to do—repent and believe the gospel! When you engage in gospel witness, however, many who listen will accuse you of arrogance and narrow-mindedness. You will be considered backward, unenlightened, politically incorrect, on the wrong side of history, and with thinking that has not sufficiently evolved. At the end of Paul's message some mocked and some believed (vv. 32–34). That will often be the case. Expect it and remain faithful to God's calling on your life.

5

When Evil Encounters Jesus

Mark 1:21–28

> 21 And they went into Capernaum, and immediately on the Sab-
> bath he entered the synagogue and was teaching. 22 And they
> were astonished at his teaching, for he taught them as one who
> had authority, and not as the scribes. 23 And immediately there
> was in their synagogue a man with an unclean spirit. And he cried
> out, 24 "What have you to do with us, Jesus of Nazareth? Have
> you come to destroy us? I know who you are—the Holy One of
> God." 25 But Jesus rebuked him, saying, "Be silent, and come out
> of him!" 26 And the unclean spirit, convulsing him and crying out
> with a loud voice, came out of him. 27 And they were all amazed,
> so that they questioned among themselves, saying, "What is this?
> A new teaching with authority! He commands even the unclean
> spirits, and they obey him." 28 And at once his fame spread every-
> where throughout all the surrounding region of Galilee.

In the desert of temptation Satan had been defeated (1:13). However, Satan is not finished in his opposition to the advancing mission of Jesus, who is now accompanied by disciples. There is a battle for the hearts of those enslaved by the evil one. We have seen that Jesus has spoken and commanded—repent, believe the gospel, and follow me. Now he commands again and performs miraculous signs to authenticate his claims, a ministry in word and deed. The disciples witness firsthand the authority of Jesus whose authority they have already responded to and the authority with which they will also engage in that mission (3:14–15; 6:7). The disciples will learn that it is not their authority but the authority of Jesus which he delegates to his people. Keep in mind that the commission the disciples received is not our commission. Our commission is that which the disciples received after the resurrection of Christ when they were re-commissioned (Matt 28:18–20). What do we learn from this encounter with evil? We assume, of course, that evil is real and active in our world today, that Satan is real and active in the world. If you cling to the misconception that people are inherently good or that each person has a spark of the divine which needs to be found and fanned, or that Satan is a comic-strip-like character replete with pitchfork, you are living in another world, a world of fantasy. What do we learn in this passage?

WE LEARN THAT TO MOVE FORWARD WITH THE GOSPEL IS TO ENCOUNTER OPPOSITION

In this passage we find Jesus teaching in the synagogue in Capernaum accompanied by the disciples he just called. Capernaum appears to have been the headquarters for this phase of Jesus' ministry. There are ruins of a second- or third-century synagogue that exist today which perhaps was built on the site of this earlier synagogue. It was a common practice for visiting teachers to be invited to speak. Fifteen times Mark mentions that Jesus taught, although here we do not know exactly what he taught.

No soul ever comes to Christ without struggle between the kingdom of darkness and the kingdom of light; no new church is ever planted without opposition as the enemy marshals his forces of evil to thwart the progress of the gospel. You should not be surprised by attacks to undermine ministry. You should remain vigilant yet confident in the authority of Christ to vanquish the enemy. Here we see the ministry of Jesus is interrupted by a demon. A few comments about demons and demon possession are in order. Demon possession is not simply another name for insanity or a primitive way to describe mental illness. It describes a condition in which a distinct and evil being (unclean spirit), foreign to the person possessed, resides in and controls that person. In the Middle Ages many believed that making the sign of the cross would expel demons. A great deal of superstition plays its role even today, and many are enamored with ministries of exorcism and find demons everywhere—demons of anger, of greed, and of lust.

As we study the New Testament, apart from the ministry of Jesus and the apostles, we do not see an ongoing emphasis on casting out demons. That leads me to believe that demon possession was limited almost exclusively to this early period in the initial advance of the kingdom announced by Jesus, the period in which the church was born. That does not mean that there are never cases in our time of demon possession, especially in regions where the gospel enters for the first time. Whatever the case may be, we are not equipped to discern the nature of a person's rebellion, their resistance to truth, or even abnormal behavior for which there may be many causes, including demonic influence. We are not obsessed with trying to determine whether or not people are demon possessed. We do not claim any special discernment to know what is going on in a person's heart or extraordinary power to cast out demons. Whatever is going on in a person's heart, it is the power of the gospel that breaks the chains which enslave the victims of Satan. When evil encounters Jesus, Jesus wins!

Christ came into the world to crush evil. We see in the Bible that there are certain things that demons know (Jas 2:19) and believe. They believe that God exists, and it causes them to tremble. Here the unclean spirit is in the presence of the Holy One and recognizes him as such in a way others do not understand, not only sinless but the one anointed for this exalted task of kingdom proclamation. The demon makes use of the man's vocal organs and asks, "Have you come to destroy us?" (v. 24). This might also be translated as an assertion: "You have come to destroy us." The One who came to seek and to save those who were lost also came to destroy the power of demons. Matthew adds another question: "Have you come to torment us before the time?" that is, before the time of final judgment (8:29). Jesus does not accept the acknowledgment of the demon. He does not need or accept the testimony of evil beings. Jesus tells the demon to be silent (muzzled) and to depart from the man. The demon obeys, unwillingly it is certain, but immediately bows to the authority of Jesus, who has struck a decisive blow. The forces of evil are in their death throes, still active, yet defeated. There is a breaking down of the reign of Satan and the establishment of God's reign.

WE LEARN THAT BEING IMPRESSED WITH JESUS' AUTHORITY IS NOT THE SAME AS BEING UNDER HIS AUTHORITY

We need to understand what this authority is which Jesus possessed and exercised. Often the words "authority" and "power" are linked. They are not necessarily the same. Authority is the right to make demands and exercise power. A vigilante mob might have the power to punish a criminal caught in the act, but they do not have the authority. Dictators might have the power to impose their will, but lack the authority. When we think of authority we think of a something imposed by a superior on an inferior (not inferior in worth but in position)—military, police, CEO, CFO, etc. All human authority is subject to whim and abuse. When we think of the authority of Jesus we need to understand that he possesses authority by virtue of who he is and he has the power to impose his will as he did with the demon. It is his authority which he has legitimately as the Son of God. The people in our text were amazed by what Jesus did. But there's no indication of submission. Why were they dumbfounded at his teaching? Because he spoke the truth, unlike the scribes who corrupted the teaching of the Old Testament (Matt 5:21–29). He spoke about matters of urgency and great significance—life, death, and eternity. The scribes often wasted their time on trivial matters (Matt 23:23). He spoke as someone concerned with the eternal welfare of his listeners. The scribes' lack of love and self-interest were well-known (Mark 12:38–40). The scribes often quoted other scribes to prove their points. Jesus spoke with authority, since his message came from God.

Those present that day understood that what happened to one demon could now be done to all. They were correct in their analysis—a new teaching with authority (or "with authority he commands"). There are many things a person can know about Jesus, can recognize about him, and still not know him nor be under his authority. It's not enough to be amazed at his teaching. You must be under his authority, which means submission, self-denial, and obedience, which are all contrary to human nature. You might be greatly impressed with Jesus and not follow him. You may find him a good man, a great teacher, and a wonderful example. You should believe those things about him, which are true. But if you go no further and refuse to bow before him as Savior and Lord, then what you believe about him is in vain.

We find later the condemnation of this city of Capernaum because of their unbelief in the face of overwhelming evidence of Jesus' identity (Matt 11:23). There are those who say even today, "If only I could see a miracle, then I would believe." Listen, those who do not believe the word of God because of the hardness of their hearts will not believe even if they see a miracle (Luke 16:31). Miracles in themselves did not bring conviction. They brought confirmation of the message, in this case the message of the arrival of the kingdom. It is not enough to be spectators or admirers of what Christ has done. It is necessary to be participants in what he is doing, engaged in mission, his mission—announcing the arrival of the king and his reign. When we respond to his authority we engage in mission by his authority. In proclaiming the gospel we confess our confidence in the power of God's word and his Spirit to defeat evil and to transform lives regardless of what is taking place in the inner being of those who hear the gospel. We are compelled to preach the gospel and stand in awe at what God does. We proclaim his victory. The power is in the word of God, not in us.

WE LEARN THAT ACCOMPANYING JESUS IS TO BE PART OF THE EXTENSION OF HIS REIGN

Jesus had already declared, "The time is fulfilled, and the kingdom of God is at hand" (Mark 1:15). He had already commanded men to follow him, just as he commands us (Mark 1:17). He now commands demons to obey him as well. Jesus is clearly extending his authority over all areas of life. There is no area of life that is not subject to him or that will not be subject to him: "For he must reign until he has put all his enemies under his feet. The last enemy that will be abolished is death . . . For this perishable body must put on the imperishable, and this mortal body must put on immortality . . . then will come about the saying that is written, 'Death is swallowed up in victory'" (1 Cor 15:25, 53–54).

We need to ask ourselves, What is the most important thing taking place in our time? Look around and look in your own life. Is it elections, sports, celebrities, economy, healthcare, pandemic, etc.? Asked in another way, where is the focus of God's activity in history? During one of my visits to Versailles in France much of the structure was covered by scaffolding. You could not see its true beauty until the scaffolding was removed. There were glimpses which the workers alone saw but were hidden to the passersby. The most significant thing in all of history is God calling out a redeemed people to be his church and to bring him glory, which begins now and will continue throughout the eternal ages. It is hidden to the eyes of the wise and self-important people of our day, hidden to those who live life as if it were theirs to live as they please and not as a gift from God. They fail to see that everything else in history is scaffolding. God is preparing his masterpiece. It cannot be seen yet for what it is and will be. As God's people we have glimpses of that. But one day God will bring down the scaffolding for all the world to see—his church, the bride of Christ, who will reign with him forever and ever! Are you part of his redeemed people? Or, asked in another way, is Jesus extending his reign over all areas of your life as you grow progressively in the knowledge of God? Let us be ready for opposition. In our lives and in our churches, we will struggle with Christ's claims as Lord while the enemy seeks to sow seeds of disruption. Let us submit to the authority of Christ, allowing him to conquer our hearts and minds. Let us be confident that Christ will prevail, ultimately and eternally.

6

The Sower and the Seed

Mark 4: 1–13

1 Again Jesus began to teach by the lake. The crowd that gathered around him was so large that he got into a boat and sat in it out on the lake, while all the people were along the shore at the water's edge. 2 He taught them many things by parables, and in his teaching said: 3 "Listen! A farmer went out to sow his seed. 4 As he was scattering the seed, some fell along the path, and the birds came and ate it up. 5 Some fell on rocky places, where it did not have much soil. It sprang up quickly, because the soil was shallow. 6 But when the sun came up, the plants were scorched, and they withered because they had no root. 7 Other seed fell among thorns, which grew up and choked the plants, so that they did not bear grain. 8 Still other seed fell on good soil. It came up, grew and produced a crop, some multiplying thirty, some sixty, some a hundred times." 9 Then Jesus said, "Whoever has ears to hear, let them hear." 10 And when he was alone, those around him with the Twelve asked him about the parables. 11 And he said to them, "To you has been given the secret of the kingdom of God, but for those outside everything is in parables, 12 so that "'they may indeed see but not perceive, and may indeed hear but not understand, lest they should turn and be forgiven.'" 13 And he said to them, "Do you not understand this parable? How then will you understand all the parables?"

This section of Mark's Gospel has been called many things—the parable of the sower, the parable of the soils, and the paradox of the kingdom of God. Up until now Mark has emphasized Jesus' teaching activity, but with little actual teaching. For the first time in this Gospel we find a substantial block of teaching. This teaching takes place in the middle of Jesus' ministry in Galilee, what has been called the First Act in the drama. Later in Mark 13 there is a second major block of Jesus' teaching in the Final Act of his ministry surrounding events in Jerusalem. Jesus continues his ministry of teaching but now in a different way. In using parables we will see some of the earlier threads now tied together to better understand the varied responses of the first three chapters. More than that, we are probed to discover how we hear the word. Jesus succeeded in drawing large crowds. Some were curious, some were eager to see miracles, but all needed to be tested in the true nature and motive for following Jesus.

One of those threads is the kingdom of God announced in 1:14–15 and not mentioned since. Crucial words are found in verse 11: "secret of the kingdom." This secret explains how the proclamation of something of such ultimate importance can be ignored or even opposed by those who hear it. In the biblical sense of the word a "secret" is not something hidden or unknowable but something previously unknown and disclosed only by revelation. This parable is a kingdom parable and the key to understanding all parables (v. 13). These parables demonstrate the various aspects of the kingdom of God, depicting his sovereign work in an unexpected manner. This also shows how the kingdom of God operates today. Those who understand this recognize the presence of salvation and the activity and power of the kingdom despite all the facts which seem to indicate the contrary.

We see in Mark the initial proclamation of the kingdom of God and the response to that message. Needless to say, that response has been varied—enthusiastic first followers, the puzzlement of those who find Jesus not following long-established traditions, the plot of the Pharisees and the Herodians to take his life, the skepticism of his own family, and the blasphemy of the scribes who attributed Jesus' miracles to Satan. These are responses to hearing the same message and seeing the same works of Jesus. How do we explain this? How do we explain that in our day this good news is not only rejected but vigorously opposed? We saw earlier that even the demons recognized that Jesus is the Holy One of God (1:24). These are the questions which this parable attempts to answer.

Parables are much more than stories that present some moral truth. They tend to puzzle as much as enlighten and are designed to shock and challenge rather than offer reassuring explanations of stories or moral platitudes. Parables are a form of speech where the meaning does not lie on the surface but demands inquiry and insight. Some commentators hold that parables make one point, in this case the ultimate harvest, although I think this is too narrow. Of course some have taken this way too far in the form of allegory. Consider Augustine's interpretation of the parable of the good Samaritan. The good Samaritan is Jesus, the traveler is Adam, Jerusalem is heaven, and Jericho is the moon, which symbolizes mortality. The robbers are the devils and his angels, the stripping of the man is depriving him of his immortality, the beating is persuading him to sin, and leaving him half dead is the effects of sin. The priest is the Jewish priesthood, the Levite is the prophets, and binding the wounds is restraint of sin. The oil is comfort and hope, the wine is encouragement to work for Christ, the donkey is the body of Christ, the inn is the church, the two coins are the two commandments to love, the innkeeper is the apostle Paul, and the return of the Samaritan is the resurrection.[1] This is a fabulous and imaginative retelling of the parable with no basis in the text or context. In fairness to Augustine, he also wrote about this parable as showing who is truly our neighbor.

To understand a parable leads to change and not merely enlightenment. The degree of communication depends on the extent the hearer shares the background of thought and values of the speaker. The meaning is not just at a cognitive level but includes a call to response in attitude, will, and action. There are elements of paradox and challenge in parables. They are an appropriate means for conveying the message of the kingdom of God which overturn some of the most basic human attitudes and values. God is not content to be an instrument in our hand or a servant at our beck and call. He is a great King and rightly makes demands on his subjects.

Although often called the parable of the sower, the sower is of relatively little importance. The focus is on the seed and on the soils on and into which the seed falls. We are called to examine our hearing of the word.

Why does the message of the kingdom meet with such mixed response? That question would've concerned Mark's readers as they observed the varying responses and should concern us today as the word goes forth. Other Scriptures deal with the relationship of human responsibility and divine sovereignty. Mark doesn't and we won't in this chapter. We hold those

1. Dodd, *Parables of the Kingdom*, 1–2.

concepts in tension since many of the answers provided go too far in one direction or another. A long time ago I stopped trying to figure out who the elect were and remain committed today to making Christ known to all, that is, sowing seed not knowing what the response will be.

Let's walk through the text with comments as we go. Keep in mind that "hearing" is the key to this passage, beginning with verse 3. The outcome of four types of seed is explained by what happens when the word is heard in verses 15, 16, 18, 20, 23, and 24. In verse 12 the emphasis is on ineffective hearing. There was seed sown "along the path." Seed was commonly ploughed in after sowing, so the seed which fell at the edge of the field was not ploughed in and remained available for the birds. This is picked up later as an indifferent hearer, someone who sees no value in what has been heard. Other seed falls on "rocky ground." Here we find impressive outward growth and inadequate roots, resulting in initial success but subsequent failure. Verses 16–17 pick this up as a symbol of the enthusiastic but unstable convert. In saying "convert" I'm not suggesting that these are genuine followers of Jesus. It is not clear that they are true believers. But Jesus' teaching and Mark's purposes do not allow us to summarily pass judgment on others. To do so would miss the point. Certainly we may form an opinion of whether someone is a genuine Christian by their conduct and their response to the word of God. But we don't always know where they are at that point in their hearing, whether the seed has been snatched away, only appears to grow, or is about to be choked off. We are called to examine ourselves, our own hearing of the word, and our own commitment to God's kingdom purposes. The seed sown on "thorny ground" did not die but was unable to produce any fruit due to competition. Notice the progression—the first seed never started, the second seed started but died, the third seed survived but could not produce grain. In the end none is of value to the farmer since he is looking for grain, not mere survival. This is picked up later as an encumbered or preoccupied follower.

As we will see, there is no indication that only one quarter of seeds proved fruitful. Mark carefully depicts the seeds and rules out the notion that those who fail are in the majority. The fate of the three seeds is described in the aorist verb tense—"eaten," "scorched," and "choked." But the seed which fell into the good ground has ongoing action in continuous growth. A threefold climax enriches the symbolism of the good seed. All true disciples are fruitful, although their fruitfulness may not be uniform. Verse 9 indicates that although everyone has ears not everyone has ears to hear. In verse 10 "those around him" is a group larger than the Twelve. To those who had this degree of curiosity to ask, more would be given. The group in this sense is self-selected, not predestined. Verses 11–12 have caused great unease and much discussion. Was there a deliberate intention to conceal the nature of the kingdom to "those outside," to keep them segregated from the disciples to whom he explained himself? Why some respond and others do not lies beyond the scope of Mark 4. Mark quotes from Isaiah 6 but reverses Isaiah's hearing and seeing to seeing and hearing. In reversing the order Mark seems to be making the point that there were those who saw what Jesus did and heard him speak. There had been equal opportunity to hear the word. Those who had initially rejected Jesus and attributed what they saw to Satan and their unwillingness to hear led to a hardening and inability to understand. Certainly it is not God's purpose to arbitrarily prevent people from understanding. If that was the case, why the command to listen, to hear?

The first three scenes describe the seed in the singular. Each scene describes the fate of a single typical seed, while in the fourth scene there are three individual seeds "yielding thirtyfold, and sixtyfold, and a hundredfold" (v. 8). Six seeds in view, three which failed and three which succeeded, which fall into the ground and produce different yields. This parable is the key to understanding all parables (v. 13). In verse 14, the "word" is the technical term for the gospel (2:2; 4:33) and we see a varying response to the gospel. This parable explains those responses in verses 14–20. In verse 15 there is immediate failure to penetrate the hard soil and the seed is lost. This ineffective hearing is attributed to the activity of Satan, who is determined to prevent the knowledge of God's kingship to be grasped. The scene in verses 16–17 is more promising initially but proves temporary. The threat to continued discipleship represented by the heat of the sun is interpreted in terms of pressure exerted on the potential disciple from the social or religious environment. These hearers "immediately receive the word with joy" and endure for a while. When persecution comes they "immediately fall away." The seed in verses 18–19 survives but is unproductive. There is no attempt to spell out here or in verse 20 what kind of fruit is expected. However, fruitful discipleship is contrasted with material concerns. It can be assumed that fruitfulness involves conformity to the principles of the kingdom of God with its opposition to societal values. The "cares of the world" are rivals to God's control. These are dangers to effective discipleship when such concerns take priority over those of the kingdom of God.

What is at issue is not affluence as such or the possession of wealth, but the attitude, the arrogance, or the independence it produces, and the enticement which threatens to seduce disciples from their true allegiance. The phrase "desires for other things" almost sounds like an "etcetera" but has the sense of superfluity or excess to capture the essence of materialism—more, more, never enough.

In verse 20 we find the final frame, where three successful seeds treated as a single group receive minimal interpretation: those who "hear the word and accept it." There is no explanation of fruit or why the difference in yield. Three different yields might be a story device to balance the three types of failures. The fruit of discipleship will not be uniform. You don't need to compare yourself and your gifts with others. We see this in the parable of the talents in Matthew 25, where equally faithful disciples are given different degrees of responsibility and produce different results. In conclusion, there are three applications. First, there is an indiscriminate sowing of the word. Why sow on soil that is not receptive? Because we don't know how it will be received. There will be negative and positive responses. There will always be a mixed reaction. Second, there is inevitable (inscrutable) rejection of the word. There are those who follow Jesus but are not followers of Jesus. Third, there is an indescribable success of the word. God's word will not return void (Isa 55:11). Our concern should be that we have gladly received the gospel and that we persevere by God's grace in fruitful Christian living.

7

If Jesus Cares About My Troubles, Why Doesn't He Do Something?

Mark 4:35–41

> 35 On that day, when evening had come, he said to them, "Let us
> go across to the other side." 36 And leaving the crowd, they took
> him with them in the boat, just as he was. And other boats were
> with him. 37 And a great windstorm arose, and the waves were
> breaking into the boat, so that the boat was already filling. 38 But
> he was in the stern, asleep on the cushion. And they woke him
> and said to him, "Teacher, do you not care that we are perishing?"
> 39 And he awoke and rebuked the wind and said to the sea, "Peace!
> Be still!" And the wind ceased, and there was a great calm. 40 He
> said to them, "Why are you so afraid? Have you still no faith?"
> 41 And they were filled with great fear and said to one another,
> "Who then is this, that even the wind and the sea obey him?"

THE "STILLING OF THE storm" continues the kingdom theme in Jesus' rebuke of the wind and waves and displays his power over nature. It also continues the theme of the disciples' struggle in understanding Jesus in their surprising behavior in response to the storm and the miracle. Instead of a request for help we find an accusing question (v. 38). This section of Mark's Gospel has four miracle stories (4:35—5:43)—nature, demons, sickness, and death. This one is the first of two nature miracles in Mark. Nature miracles establish Jesus' authority over inanimate creation just as the healings show his authority over animate creation. Nature miracles show that Jesus is Lord over all, over individuals and over creation. Mark most likely received this story from Peter or other witnesses with the attention to incidental details (other boats, cushion). The next section begins with another lake miracle, Jesus walking on the water (6:45). Some see this as six miracle stories with 6:45 ending the section with Jesus' appearance on the sea answering the disciples' question in 4:41, "Who then is this, that even the wind and the sea obey him?" Let's look at several elements in this narrative.

THERE WAS A GREAT STORM

We see the serenity of Jesus in the midst of disaster emphasized with mention of a "cushion" on which Jesus lay his head and of which Peter was an eyewitness. Mark describes the windstorm in language which reminds us of Jonah. It was a howling tempest, a violent upheaval. Many have compared the sleeping of Jesus with that of Jonah. The parallel cannot be avoided. Yet in Jesus' sleeping we see a stark contrast with the raging storm. We see his confidence in the Father and also his humanity. The word "asleep" at the end of the sentence in Greek creates a dramatic effect, a contrast with the disciples' fear. There are not only similarities with Jonah but sharp contrasts. Of course Jonah's sleeping was during his attempt to escape his mission. Differences between Jonah and Jesus emerge even more clearly in the response to the storm. Yet the parallel continues further with Jonah's captain awaking him and accusing him of dereliction of duty. Jesus' companions awaken him questioning his concern for their survival. The catastrophic proportions of the storm can be felt with each crashing wave filling the ship. The disciples may have been frantically bailing out the ship but to no avail. The disciples' question is a rebuke of Jesus. "Don't you care?" The rebuke also may've implied "Do something!"

Perspective reminds us that although there are storms in life which may cause us to question God's concern for us, not all that we consider storms really are. We are tempted at times to call God's care for us into question for things that are mere inconveniences or annoyances. We all think we know people like that but rarely think it is us. We are easily given to drama and should exercise care in dealing with the events and annoyances of life. We often carry those dramas into our interpersonal relationships, where it doesn't take much to set us off, either questioning God or complaining to others about our lives.

Certainly there are life-threatening illnesses, the prospect of financial ruin, and the pain of broken relationships. Yes, the storms of life are real, and we are reminded that we are not in control. Here was something life-threatening. Our problem is that we either think we are in control of our lives or are seeking to control our lives or the lives of others. We want God to march to our tune and others as well. We need to learn: I am not in control, of myself, of others, or of God. You can sing all you want with Frank Sinatra, "I Did It My Way," but your way is never the right way. Proverbs 14:12 tells us that man's way is the way of death.

THERE WAS A GREAT CALM

The words of Jesus demonstrate the authority of Jesus over the chaotic powers of nature. It's as if he were addressing an unruly heckler—"Be quiet! Shut up." The words translated "rebuke" and "be still" were used in Mark 1:25 with an exorcism in casting out a demon. Jesus' response indicates that the disciples should have shown great trust in him, not cowardice, and he rebuked them. Their fear exposed a lack of faith. But what does Jesus mean by "faith" here? Perhaps the best way is to see this as trust in "God's helping power present and active in Jesus." The words "not yet" suggest that something was lacking that could or should have been expected. Jesus had already questioned them in 4:13 and will later in 7:18. The disciples still did not understand the issue in the previous parables—the presence of God's sovereign rule in Jesus' person and ministry in spite of appearances to the contrary. Even after an explanation they did not understand the parables. Fear of the storm overwhelmed their commitment to Jesus. Jesus shows them that their fear was unfounded. Their faith should have assured them of their safety even without a miracle, since Jesus was sleeping serenely.

There is a tension in Mark's portrayal of the disciples who had received a special calling, who had a privileged relationship with Jesus, and had received special instruction in the interpretation of the parables. This by no means suggests that they were unbelievers. The disciples were much like us. We see ourselves in them, in our halting and feeble trust. We are rebuked, but with the Savior it is a loving reproach to prod us in our understanding of his ways, and lacking understanding, a trust in him. It may be that the community Mark was writing to was struggling with reconciling the way of the cross, persecution, and suffering, and needed this reminder that Christ was powerfully at work in the world. They might not always experience miraculous deliverance, but they could have confidence nonetheless in the presence and power of Jesus who would never leave them nor forsake them. The parallels with Jonah show Jesus to be greater than Jonah (Matt 12:41). Instead of praying to God as Jonah did, Jesus personally addresses the wind and the sea. In doing so he accomplished what in the Old Testament only God could do in the midst of chaos.

THERE WAS GREAT FEAR

The story concludes by showing the disciples "filled with fear" (lit. "feared a great fear"). This was their response to the miracle. The word translated "fear" (v. 41), a reverential awe that is greater than any fear of a storm, is different from the one translated "afraid" (v. 40). This is the appropriate response of humans faced with a display of divine power. They were looking to Jesus for something, but the scale of his action overwhelmed them. Jonah 1:10 in the Septuagint (LXX), the Greek translation of the Old Testament, has the same expression, "feared a great fear," employed by Jonah's companions. A similar expression is used in 1:16 in their response to the calming of the sea after Jonah had been thrown overboard, a response that led to sacrifice and prayers. The disciples had already known personal abuse in their association with Jesus and were facing the prospect of persecution. They needed to know, as do we, that although Jesus may not always appear present or to care, we should not be in doubt that he is present and at work in our lives.

The disciples ask a question that everyone should ask. "Who then is this?" For these disciples, the question does not express confusion but amazement and astonishment. This is Jesus, the one whom even the wind and the waves obey, even when storms overwhelm us, and it seems that God is not at work in our lives or situation. The question of Jesus' identity is not answered here but later in 8:29 when Peter confesses, "You are the Christ!" You and I are left to answer on the basis of the story. How do you answer this question? If Jesus is the exalted King, at work in the world and bringing all things to the Father's desired end, more powerful than evil and in control of nature, what does that mean for your life today, for your trust in him? Are you ready to relinquish control of that which you can't control anyway and trust, truly trust him, daily trust him?

8

What Does God Want Most From Me?

Mark 12:28–34

> 28 And one of the scribes came up and heard them disputing
> with one another, and seeing that he answered them well, asked
> him, "Which commandment is the most important of all?" 29 Je-
> sus answered, "The most important is, 'Hear, O Israel: The Lord
> our God, the Lord is one. 30 And you shall love the Lord your
> God with all your heart and with all your soul and with all your
> mind and with all your strength.' 31 The second is this: 'You shall
> love your neighbor as yourself.' There is no other commandment
> greater than these." 32 And the scribe said to him, "You are right,
> Teacher. You have truly said that he is one, and there is no other
> besides him. 33 And to love him with all the heart and with all the
> understanding and with all the strength, and to love one's neigh-
> bor as oneself, is much more than all whole burnt offerings and
> sacrifices." 34 And when Jesus saw that he answered wisely, he said
> to him, "You are not far from the kingdom of God." And after that
> no one dared to ask him any more questions.

Who can love in this way? The bent of our hearts goes in another direction. "Jesus loves me, so do I, I love me, and so should you." When I read our text, I alternate between despair and delight, delight in the lofty ideal of this kind of love and despair in falling short. This is wonderful! This is impossible! I can't do this and neither can you on your own. You can't work this up on your own or work this out from inside. Yet God does not command what he will not empower. What is impossible for you to accomplish is not impossible for God to accomplish in you. It won't happen all at once. You won't wake up tomorrow and have this fixed. But this is encouraging. In the midst of hostility and opposition we finally see a genuine seeker. This is the only time where Jesus commends a scribe. In previous verses the scribes were part of the opposition. In the following verses Jesus will warn about the scribes. Here is someone who comes with an honest question. Something about Jesus has attracted him.

The scribes had identified 613 commandments. They were divided into "heavy" and "light" commands, from most important to least important. There were numerous attempts to summarize God's commands since most people would not memorize a list of 613 commandments, 248 positive and 365 negative. Hillel, a well-known Jewish teacher in the first century AD, reportedly summarized the law in this way while standing on one leg: "What is hateful to you, do not to your neighbor; that is the whole Torah, while the rest is commentary." It was a way of saying that although all God's commands are important, some are fundamental or foundational from which the others arise. These commandments reflect the two tables of the Decalogue (Ten Commandments), the first book dealing primarily with our vertical relationship with God; the second dealing with our horizontal relationship with others. How can we love in this way? What do we need to know about this love?

LOVING GOD AND YOUR NEIGHBOR IN THIS WAY IS POSSIBLE ONLY IN A COVENANTAL RELATIONSHIP WITH HIM

Loving God and others begins with a call to worship as in Deuteronomy 6:4–5. "Hear, O Israel: The LORD our God, the LORD is one. You shall love the LORD your God with all your heart and with all your soul and with all your might." This call to worship was given to the people of God when they left Egypt. It was based on the nature of God, his oneness as the basis of monotheism. Because he is one, our love for him must be undivided. Mark's readers, like many early Christians, had no doubt been accused of being polytheists. Jesus affirms the oneness of God and at the same time asserts that he is God the Son. One God in three persons. This command is not the means to enter into a relationship with God or into the community but obedience to this command results from a relationship with him.

God doesn't want your obedience without your love. If he has your love the obedience will follow. We love him because he first loved us (1 John 4:19).

Loving God and others is not a natural impulse. By nature we are egotistical and self-centered. We love ourselves. Who have you loved this week? I loved me. You loved you. Why does God set the standard so high? 1) Because he can't do otherwise. The word "all" is repeated four times; 2) Because he wants us to see our inability to obey apart from grace; 3) Because he wants us to understand that this love is not simply a feeling or sentiment that we can work up. It is a radical reshaping of our entire being, one that begins at conversion and continues throughout the Christian life. We never come to the point where we have fulfilled this command. The reference to heart, soul, mind, and strength is a way of speaking of your entire life and being. We can speak of affections, desires, thinking, and energy, but the point is not to separate these actions but to see them as a whole.

This command will lay a foundation for your obedience to all the rest. Loving God with all your heart will guard you from things that are rivals to his reign in your life, will engage you in activities by which he may be honored and with which he will be pleased. The apostle John tells us that God's commands are not burdensome (1 John 5:3). There are things we must resist and that we must not do because they are inconsistent with our declared love for God. God is one and our hearts must be one with him, and since there is no God besides him, no rival must be admitted into our lives to compete with him.

LOVING GOD AND YOUR NEIGHBOR MUST BE PRACTICED IN THE CONTEXT OF COMMUNITY

Leviticus 19:18 tells us, "You shall not take vengeance or bear a grudge against the sons of your own people, but you shall love your neighbor as yourself: I am the LORD." This command is repeated several times in the New Testament (Matt 19:19; Gal 5:14; Jas 2:8; Rom 13:8–10).

Apart from a covenant relationship with God through Christ, you know only that you must obey God's commands, but you find that you cannot do what he commands in your own strength or by sheer willpower. You can know a great deal about love or think you do but it may remain abstract or deformed. You cannot love God apart from participating in a community of believers and loving his people, his church. In a day where for many the church has become irrelevant and/or optional we must constantly reaffirm our commitment to honor what God has instituted and to participate in a community of the redeemed where we gather for corporate worship. You might find some people easier to love than others. God doesn't give you the option of picking and choosing who you should love. First John 3:14 says, "We know that we have passed out of death into life, because we love the brothers. Whoever does not love abides in death."

In the above-quoted Old Testament passage, neighbors were fellow Israelites and foreigners who lived among them. Jesus redefines "neighbor." Jesus enlarged the Old Testament idea of neighbor and included enemies, Samaritans, and Gentiles. The great commandment has two sides—loving God and loving our neighbor. In vain we declare our love for God when it is divorced from love for our neighbor. In the parable of the good Samaritan (Luke 10:25–37), a man was beaten and robbed, and when a priest and Levite saw him, they "passed by on the other side" (10:31–32). Only a despised Samaritan had compassion on him and showed him kindness (10:33). Jesus told the story in response a lawyer's question, "Who is my neighbor?" (10:29). The lawyer was looking more for justification of his actions than an answer. If you ask, "Who is my neighbor?" you have already demonstrated your lack of love for God in trying to limit your obligation to love others. If you ask this question, then you are not neighborly. Jesus asked, "Which of these three, do you think, proved to be a neighbor to the man who fell among the robbers?" (10:36). The lawyer rightly responded, "The one who showed him mercy." When you gather publicly with God's people, the place is filled with your neighbors who need mercy. I am your neighbor. The person next to you is your neighbor. Show mercy as evidence of your love for your neighbor.

How about loving "your neighbor as yourself?" (v. 31). How do we understand that? This phrase at first glance puzzles us. Does Jesus advocate self-love? To love others as you love yourself is not an encouragement to self-love. We need no encouragement for this. The statement simply recognizes what is generally true. There may be some people who practice self-loathing, but most people love themselves in caring for real or perceived needs. The commands to love God and love our neighbor are inseparable. One without the other leaves us unbalanced, either with religious mysticism or fleeting sentimentalism. You will need this love for neighbor in your community, for one another, for church leaders, and for those you are trying to reach with the gospel. You can be sure that there will be times of disappointment and the potential for division. The more diverse a church is, the greater the potential for divisions and misunderstandings. You may have grown up distrustful, fearful, or resentful of people of other races or ethnicities. You may have entered the Christian life with a well-defined set of prejudices that are undermined by the gospel and need to be dismantled. You may have homeless people in your church alongside homeowners, law breakers and law enforcers, highly educated professionals and high school dropouts. Loving your neighbor as yourself sounds great in theory but is a daily struggle where you need to surrender to God's grace, confess your failings, and take steps that actually demonstrate your love for others. It may be meeting a real financial need. It may be helping a college student stay in school. It may be a hospital or prison visit. It may be sitting at a table with someone you do not know and asking about their story of God's work in their lives and telling yours.

NEARNESS TO THE KINGDOM IS STILL OUTSIDE THE KINGDOM AND INCAPABLE OF THIS LOVE

The scribe who asked Jesus about the greatest commandment was "not far from the kingdom of God" (v. 34). This scribe was in the presence of the One who had inaugurated the kingdom of God. He understands the meaning and spirit of Jesus' teaching. He knows the way into the kingdom but has not yet entered. You also can be close, encouraged to enter, and still remain outside. Yet there was hope for this man if he acted on the light he had received. If he goes as far as he can with the light he has then God's grace will carry him further, into the kingdom. We don't know what this scribe did. Where are you, in the kingdom or outside looking in? What will you do? Attending church and a concern for spiritual matters are good things. You are at least near to the kingdom, perhaps as a seeker as this scribe was. Jesus invites you into his kingdom and wants to reign over your life. You cannot love God and others if you are near but not actually in the kingdom.

As a Christian, does the text leave you wanting more in your relationship with God and others? The text should not lead us to despair, although initially God's word is like a hammer on our heart. His word is also a balm for our souls. The text should lead us to turn to God in humble daily devotion and dependence, to daily confess where we fail, and to earnestly look to Christ for the strength we can never find in ourselves to love God, who is altogether lovely, and then turn to our neighbors who sometimes are altogether unlovely. "For he who does not love his brother whom he has seen cannot love God whom he has not seen" (1 John 4:20). Loving God and others must not be half-hearted or self-centered, or for special occasions when we feel it. It is a way of life to be embraced. Embrace that life and allow God to nurture in you a greater love for him and for others that is not in word only but in deed and in truth.

9

Don't Drift Away

Hebrews 2:1–4

> 1 Therefore we must pay much closer attention to what we have heard, lest we drift away from it. 2 For since the message declared by angels proved to be reliable, and every transgression or disobedience received a just retribution, 3 how shall we escape if we neglect such a great salvation? It was declared at first by the Lord, and it was attested to us by those who heard, 4 while God also bore witness by signs and wonders and various miracles and by gifts of the Holy Spirit distributed according to his will.

THERE IS A PAINTING on display at the Naval History Museum in Mexico City. It depicts an event from 1519 when Hernando Cortez, a ruthless, haughty conquistador, scuttled his ships at Veracruz to prevent his soldiers from returning to Spain. When I think about the message of Hebrews and the challenges which believers faced in the first century, the story of Cortez comes to mind. Imagine the soldiers standing on the beach watching their only means of departure sinking to the bottom of the Gulf of Mexico. It was a visible illustration that there was no turning back, there was no standing still, there was only one direction in which to move—forward. These men might've been tempted to return to Spain, to the safety they enjoyed, to their families. But now they stood uncertain as to what lay ahead as they moved inland away from the coast, away from their only means of escape. Many of them would never return to Spain. They died in the jungles and in battle.

We find a parallel with the Christian life. We may be tempted to return to what we left behind when we are faced with the uncertainty of what lies ahead, and when we find that the Christian life has its share of struggles and disappointments. Be honest, have you not at times thought that life was easier before you became a Christian, or you thought life would be better than it is as a Christian? Maybe no one told you that the Christian life might be difficult.

I've been a Christian for almost fifty years. I look back over that time and often think of people I know who were with me in college, or in churches, members and even pastors of churches, who no longer go to church, who don't read the Bible anymore, who no longer have time for God in their lives, who raised their children and grandchildren without pointing them to Jesus. That could happen to you or to me. You will be disappointed at times in your Christian life. It might be with people, it might be with your pastors or your church, or it might be with God. It might be a relationship with a young man or young woman that you treasure more than you treasure Christ. Others begin to dictate what you do on Sundays or how you live your life. Satan will use any means to draw you away from God and from the only true security you have in life. It doesn't always happen quickly. Sometimes it's like being on a raft or boat in the water where the current moves you slowly until you suddenly find yourself in danger. It's a dangerous place to be.

This book tells us that for the true child of God there is no turning back. Once you have known the joy of the forgiveness of sins, fellowship with the Eternal God, peace which passes all understanding, and grace upon grace, you may look back but you can't turn back. Jesus said, "No one who puts his hand to the plow and looks back is fit for the kingdom of God" (Luke 9:62). To turn back would invite the judgment of God. To turn back would be disastrous and in fact an indication that maybe you never truly experienced new life in Christ. You may be disappointed, no, you *will* be at times in the Christian life and in people. You may doubt God's truth and promises when attacked by skeptics, and you might be pressured into political and religious correctness. But you can't turn back. The author tells us to look to Jesus, the Founder and Perfecter of our faith (Heb 12:2), in whom "we may receive mercy and find grace to help in time of need" (Heb 4:16).

One of the overarching themes of Hebrews is that Christ is "better," "more excellent," "greater," or "superior" than anything or anyone the readers might have heard, known, or experienced. Christ is superior to angels

(1:2), possesses more glory than Moses (3:2), offers a Sabbath rest for God's people (4:9), is declared an eternal high priest after the order of Melchizedek (5:6), is the guarantor of a better covenant (7:22), has obtained a more excellent ministry than Old Testament priests (8:8), and provides a better, once-for-all sacrifice for sins (9:23, 26; 10:12). Believers are promised a better and abiding possession (10:34) and now desire a "better country, that is, a heavenly one" (11:16) with the promise of a better resurrection (11:35). Hebrews demonstrates the incomparable superiority and the finality of God's work in Jesus Christ. It presents the conviction that Christianity is thus absolute and universal in scope. The author writes to warn and exhort Christians to remain faithful in the face of opposition and for what would be for many the certainty of persecution and even martyrdom. He's warning us: don't drift from the gospel and don't drift from Christ who is the only secure anchor for your soul. Here are the reasons.

THERE IS A FINAL, AUTHORITATIVE WORD FROM GOD WE NEED TO HEAR AND THERE WILL BE NO OTHER

In chapter 1 of Hebrews we are not told to do anything—no commands, no exhortation. The first chapter presents and proclaims God's final and decisive word to the world, Jesus Christ the Son of God. God has spoken in Jesus and points to Jesus, who possesses the fullness of God and majesty of God. Only after presenting the exalted Christ in chapter 1 do we find the first command in Hebrews—"pay much closer attention to what we have heard" (2:1). What we have heard surely refers to the whole Christian gospel. To "pay attention" to what we have heard is to act upon it. It's possible to hear without paying attention, as children and husbands often do. The superiority of Jesus Christ provides the incentive to honor and worship him supremely. Although times have changed, the dangers facing Christians remain. There is much to fascinate you in this world. There are many things to distract you from an intense focus on Jesus Christ and from a determined commitment to his purposes. Social media captures your attention, and many television programs and commercials are designed to indoctrinate you to accept the world's perversions, to show you how happy people are who live in violation of God's creation design for heterosexual and monogamous marriage between a man and a woman (Gen 2). There are varied voices to seduce you, to sow doubt in your mind, to intimidate you into silence. There is pressure to conform, whether dictatorial as in the first century or political in the twenty-first century, and it must be resisted. These Christians underwent persecution (Heb 10:32). They had paid a price for their faith. Now some of them were wavering. They needed to hear what we need to have repeated in our day. Where God has spoken we pay attention and we bring our opinions into conformity to his revelation. We refuse to bow the knee to Caesar regardless of the form government takes. We refuse to accommodate the uprising against biblical morality. We refuse to provide entertainment to people and call it church. Many churches are falling over themselves to see who can be the most welcoming and affirming of so-called alternate lifestyles. They boast about it on their websites. The church where I serve, Grace Church of Philly, is welcoming and loves those of all lifestyles. We will not deny people the right to make choices even if we believe those choices are harmful and contrary to God's word. Neither will we use coercive measures to bring about change. But we will not affirm what God condemns. We will not say, "It doesn't matter, it's all okay."

There are rival voices for your loyalty. Who do you listen to? We all listen to someone or something even if it's the little voice in our head. It might be the political pundits, the celebrity crowd, the politicians, the intellectuals, radio personalities, and the media. Weigh all voices by the one authoritative voice of God's word. Will you listen to the new atheists, who sound much like the old atheists? Will you listen to the new morality which sounds like the old immorality? The author reminds us early on that the glory and splendor of this world system are fading away (1:10–12) and that true satisfaction cannot be found apart from conscious fellowship with Jesus Christ. He is the heir of all things, worshiped by the angels, he is God whose throne is forever and ever. As F. F. Bruce put it so clearly, "As God has no greater messenger than his Son, he has no greater message than the gospel."[1]

THERE IS A REAL DANGER OF DRIFTING AWAY FROM THE REFUGE OF THE GOSPEL

We find in Hebrews a series of five warnings. Warnings are good when they are for our benefit. Parents tell their children, "don't run out in the street, don't touch a pan on a hot stove, don't talk to or get in a car with strangers." Lifeguards tell you to stay close to shore because of riptides. Signs are posted warning of danger. That doesn't mean all warnings are good or true,

1. Bruce, *Hebrews*, 65.

like if you cross your eyes they might get stuck that way. But the warnings in the Bible are good for us and they are true.

This is the first of the five warnings in Hebrews. Commentators debate to whom these warnings are directed and whether the consequences are eternal or temporal. Some believe that the consequences seem so severe that unbelievers who reject the gospel are in view. Others believe that Christians are being addressed and warned about apostasy—falling away from grace and as a result losing their salvation. It seems to me that among the recipients of this letter, in the churches, there would be both believers and professing believers, those genuinely born again and those loosely and superficially attached to Christianity without the reality of union with Christ. If there is no fruit, no faithfulness, no progressive transformation of life, then there should be a fearful consideration of where you stand with God, whether you have ever truly known him and experienced his glorious salvation. It is possible to be connected to the Christian community in a superficial way. You might attend church week after week or even be a church member and not really know the Lord. What we do know is this: No one who has ever genuinely repented of their sins and turned to Christ for salvation will ever be lost. No one can pluck them out of the Son's or Father's hand (John 10:27–29). What we also know is that true believers can grow cold and indifferent. They can neglect this "great salvation" to the point where divine discipline becomes inevitable (Heb 12:7) and in the hand of a loving Father the means to bring them back to experience the joy of their salvation.

This first warning is the danger of "drifting away" or, as the King James Version puts it, "let it slip." This word was used both of drifting away in a boat or a ring slipping off a finger. The picture of drifting is of someone slowly and in some ways unconsciously moving away from the refuge of the gospel. It is not only violent opposition to the gospel that brings loss but drifting away as well. Yes, the loss is very different between an unbeliever who drifts by the gospel and never seizes it and the believer who moves away from what he has embraced. For an unbeliever, the loss is eternal. Yet for believers the temporal loss is real—the failure to accomplish God's purposes in their lives, the loss of opportunities for the furtherance of the gospel in advancing their own agendas. We only have one life to live for Christ. There were some among the recipients of this epistle already slipping away, according to Hebrews 10:25, "not neglecting to meet together, as is the habit of some, but encouraging one another, and all the more as you see the Day drawing near." You can't live the Christian life in isolation. You can't grow as a disciple apart from the community of faith. You are either standing firm in Jesus or drifting away from him. The word of God calls us to what John Piper calls "joyful vigilance." We do not moan and complain that we have to listen to what God has said. We rejoice that God has called us by his grace and made us partakers of his glory in Jesus.

An old expression "put on the shelf" was used to describe Christians who drifted away and no longer faithfully served and followed their Lord. Another term was "backslider" to describe those who once lived the Christian life but went backward and were living in sin or seemed indifferent to spiritual realities. Some may debate the appropriateness of these expressions. The Scriptures, however, do not allow us to find comfort or offer assurance of salvation to anyone not presently living under the lordship of Christ. Yes, we all experience his lordship imperfectly. Yes, we all sin and stand daily in need of forgiveness. Yes, we all stand by grace alone and the merits of Christ and never our own merits. Yet there should be great concern when there is a pattern, whether of perpetual indifference or passive rebellion against the Lord and his commands, when the word of God no longer brings conviction, when we find it easy to avoid corporate worship for trivialities, and when our hearts are not captured by freedom in Christ but enslaved to sin. False profession is a real danger. We cannot summarily dismiss warnings and find refuge in affirming "once saved always saved" and the biblical teaching of justification by faith. These affirmations are true. The warnings also are real. Hebrews roots our objective confidence in Christ and in his completed work on the cross. He lived the perfect life we could not live and died the death we deserved. He rose again and reigns today at the right hand of the Father. Salvation is God's work in which we do not cooperate. We receive salvation by grace through faith alone. At the same time, our experience of this work must be expressed in new life in Christ, at times with only faint glimmers, always with struggle in recognition of our weakness and failures, yet moving on in the right direction because our hearts are set on following Christ. Romans 8:1 tells us, "There is therefore now no condemnation to those who are in Christ Jesus." Yet it would be folly to imagine that praying the sinners' prayer requires nothing more in someone's life—no transformation, no love for God, his word, his people—until they safely arrive in heaven. Your profession of faith does not save you and can actually mislead you if unaccompanied by new life in Christ. We believe in the assurance of salvation and the present possession of eternal life. We also believe that knowing Christ as Savior can never be divorced from serving him as Lord.

We all struggle at times with the tendency to do the minimum, to resist change or resist allowing God to change us, to grow us. Sometimes it is not active disobedience but neglect. Like a garden, it doesn't need to be trampled to die. Simple neglect will do. Or like a house. Years of neglect will accomplish what a wrecking ball can do, except the wrecking ball does it more quickly. The fact that you struggle with sin and temptation is in fact a good sign. Struggle is a sign of life. It indicates that the Spirit of God is at work. It is a work that will continue until death or when Jesus returns. But make no mistake. If you drift you cannot escape judgment. The law was given in the presence and by the mediation of angels. Disobedience brought God's disfavor. God has now spoken in his glorious Son. Disobey him at your own peril.

THERE IS A GENERATION TO FOLLOW WHICH NEEDS A FAITHFUL TESTIMONY TODAY

In other words, there are both immediate and future consequences for our spiritual failures or spiritual faithfulness. We see that these readers were second-generation Christians. Even the author seems to indicate that he was not among the original apostles but had these things confirmed to him. This message was first declared by the Lord, then attested to others by the first audience. God had borne witness to the truth of the message by signs, wonders, and miracles. There was no expectation that these signs would continue after the time of the apostles. What would continue was the people of God, a faithful witness, an often persecuted but enduring witness. Hebrews 11 recounts a long list of faithful witnesses, many who gave their lives in identifying with the one true God. That witness is alive and under attack today. More Christians were martyred in the twentieth century than all the previous centuries combined, and the twenty-first century shows no reprieve. We may not be called to martyrdom, but we are called to take seriously what we have heard, to live it, to propagate it, and at all times, as Jude tells us, to "contend for the faith which was once for all delivered to the saints" (v. 3). And we are called to encourage one another to love and do good works. That doesn't happen when we are so wrapped up in our own lives and when we substitute our ambitions for God's purposes. Our generation needs a faithful witness, to see people who are serious about being disciples of Jesus Christ. If Jesus doesn't return in our generation, there will be another generation. How are you contributing to that next generation?

Now the hard and unavoidable questions. In what ways might you be neglecting such a great salvation? What so occupies your life and interests that you are easily distracted from spiritual pursuits, from fellowship with God's people? How will you escape if you continue to neglect what you have heard? You won't. You can't. But you can turn to Christ, the one for whom your neglect has really been rejection of his gracious offer of salvation; or the one for whom your neglect has been a slow drift away from living the truth you embrace. For one and all there is a refuge that will hold you secure even when you can't hold on. There's grace for sinners. There's grace for saints. Don't drift away!

10

Surviving Another Year

Philippians 3:7–14

> 7 But whatever gain I had, I counted as loss for the sake of Christ.
> 8 Indeed, I count everything as loss because of the surpassing
> worth of knowing Christ Jesus my Lord. For his sake I have suf-
> fered the loss of all things and count them as rubbish, in order that
> I may gain Christ 9 and be found in him, not having a righteous-
> ness of my own that comes from the law, but that which comes
> through faith in Christ, the righteousness from God that depends
> on faith— 10 that I may know him and the power of his resurrec-
> tion, and may share his sufferings, becoming like him in his death,
> 11 that by any means possible I may attain the resurrection from
> the dead. 12 Not that I have already obtained this or am already
> perfect, but I press on to make it my own, because Christ Jesus has
> made me his own. 13 Brothers, I do not consider that I have made
> it my own. But one thing I do: forgetting what lies behind and
> straining forward to what lies ahead, 14 I press on toward the goal
> for the prize of the upward call of God in Christ Jesus.

If you are reading this today it's because you survived another year by God's grace and in his plan for your life. Perhaps you survived COVID-19 or recovered from illness or an accident. Perhaps you lost loved ones and still live with grief. You look back on last year with some regret and some sorrow. If you're like many people, every January you make resolutions to experience change in your life. Someone defined a resolution as a "decision that you probably won't keep and you will soon forget." We hear about principles of success, secrets of victorious living, ways to lose weight, or how to succeed in the new year. We are given three steps for this, three principles for that, three keys to open the right doors, to get what you want, to be what you want to be. For most people it doesn't take long to fall off the "resolution wagon." I'm not going to ask you to make a resolution after reading this chapter. I will ask you to seriously consider whether you will merely survive this year and the next or if you will thrive. Of course, I'm particularly concerned about thriving spiritually, although God may bless and prosper in other ways. But if you thrive economically, educationally, or in any other way this year but do not thrive spiritually, you risk wasting another year. You need something, or better, Someone, to sustain you in your journey, in your pilgrimage toward the holy city that will be your future and permanent dwelling place. As you live this out, where do you want to be found more faithful twelve months from now—church life, personal walk with God, personal evangelism, family life, employment, education? The beginning of a year is a good time to audit our hearts for our hidden places of faithlessness. But any time is really a good time. Today is the best time. What have you neglected or excused? What might God finally remove from your life, or bring back to life?

It is good to look back over past years as long as you don't camp there in regret. It is good to think about this year as long as you don't create unrealistic expectations that will bring disappointment. We realize that we have little control over many temporary outcomes in our lives. We have no guarantee of success defined by us in following the right steps. We do have assurance of ultimate outcomes based on the promises of God. Perhaps you entered this year with a past year or years of spiritual lethargy and defeat. For that there is no quick fix, but there is hope. You may have entered the new year with a past year of spiritual growth and victorious living. For that to continue there will be new challenges to face and new enemies to defeat. Your defeat does not prevent you from living this year restored in fellowship with God and his people. Your spiritual success doesn't count for what God expects of you and wants to do in your life this year. It doesn't matter how many New Years you have seen (and some of us have seen many), there's always more to be done. Some people are challenged to think how they would live this year if they knew it was their last year. Would they read their Bible more, witness more, attend church more, give more? Maybe. But since we don't know what the future holds, those thoughts often remain in the realm of the imagination. Paul said he died every day (1 Cor 15:31). Proverbs tells us to not boast about tomorrow because we don't know "what a day may bring" (27:1).

What we need to ask is how should we live today. I don't know that we should go around like it's our last day and try to do everything we think we should do. If it was the last day there's not enough time to do everything on the bucket list or what needs to be done. But every day is a gift from God, and we do well to seek to live each day for him and his glory. This past year had some surprises, didn't it, some things you didn't see coming? Some of you had loved ones pass into the presence of the Lord. Some of your friends and loved ones were stricken with life-threatening illnesses. Some of you had and still have serious health concerns. This present year and next year may be no different. So, I'm not trying to live as if it was my last year on earth. I'd like to think that I want to live each day as God wants me to live it. The truth is that I don't consciously think of it in that way every day. That's why along with our daily walk with the Lord we need to gather as God's people and with God's people. That's why we observe the Lord's Supper weekly in our church, to be reminded of what Christ has done for us, to repent of our sin, and to be refreshed by God's grace. When you commit yourself to that way of life you can't or shouldn't remain the same. Keep in mind these twin truths: You can't focus on Christ and remain unchanged. You can't love God with all your heart and hold on to your idolatrous ways.

Spiritual renewal is something God does in us. But we are not passive. We don't sit back and let it happen. Paul said, "But by the grace of God I am what I am, and his grace toward me was not in vain. On the contrary, I worked harder than any of them, though it was not I, but the grace of God that is with me" (1 Cor 15:10). There is effort on your part. If you want to read the Bible more or pray more you need to discipline yourself to set aside time to do it. If you want to grow more in your knowledge of God's word, you need to take advantage of opportunities to study it provided by your church. For some Christians it will mean less time on Facebook, less time in front of the television, more consistent attendance at church services, or giving more to the work of God. Many of these areas of our lives begin to resolve themselves when our priorities are right, when we live according to God's principles and "seek first the kingdom of God" (Matt 6:33). We meet people all the time who were born into a religion but need to be born again in Christ. Encountering Christ changed everything for Paul and put his past, present, and future into perspective. Our relationship with Christ will do the same for us. These are not quick steps. These are realities that will bring renewal and spiritual refreshment in your life. Here are several commitments to help you grow in Christ by God's grace.

YOU NEED TO GRASP THE INCOMPARABLE VALUE OF BELONGING TO AND BEING IN CHRIST

Paul speaks of gaining Christ (v. 8) and being found in him (v. 9). In the first six verses before our text we see Paul's starting point for a renewed cross-centered and Christ-centered life. Paul viewed his ancestry and past spiritual accomplishments as without value in being rightly related to God. He had no control over his ancestry. He made religious choices which were consistent with his background and upbringing. He makes a distinction between the Judaizers (circumcised in their flesh) and the true circumcision (circumcised in their hearts). Genuine believers are those who worship by the Spirit of God and not by human traditions or external ritual, who glory in Christ with satisfaction in knowing that their hope is in Christ alone, and who have no confidence in the flesh, knowing that in their sinful humanity they are separated from Christ.

Paul declared that "whatever gain" (v. 7) he had in his past life apart from Christ was now counted as loss (liabilities). He moves from "whatever gain" counted as loss to "everything" and "all things" (v. 8) counted as loss in which he might place his confidence. This is genuine conversion. Paul contrasts the old life and the new life. We don't need our lives adjusted or something added to them. When we come to Christ something radical takes place. There is loss and there is death: loss of what we considered valuable in the eyes of God to earn his favor; death to the old life and new life in Christ. Paul's influence, prestige, and law-obedience were all in the loss column. Christ is seen now as the ultimate "gain" (v. 7). We also see progression in how Paul views his conversion, for "the sake of Christ" (v. 7), for the "surpassing worth of knowing Christ" (v. 8), in order to "gain Christ" (v. 8b), to be found in Christ (v. 9). This reminds us of the words of Jesus in Matthew 16:26, "For what will it profit a man if he gains the whole world and forfeits his soul? Or what shall a man give in return for his soul?"

Regeneration, this new life in Christ, is the beginning of the discovery of the riches of God's great salvation. Take time to look back to the day you were saved. How much of your life has experienced transformation, and how are you growing in the riches of Christ, in whom are "hidden the treasures of wisdom and knowledge" (Col. 2:3)? Maybe when you became a Christian you were initially excited about what God had done and you wanted to tell people about Christ. Are you still excited and wanting to tell others about Jesus? Ask yourself what has really changed in your life, or what needs to change. What Paul once considered spiritual assets he now considers liabilities, described as dung or manure, or what was thrown to the dogs. The emphasis is not on revulsion but on worthlessness. Paul did not despise his heritage or oppose the acquisition of knowledge. For us, it is not a question of denying our heritage and human achievements as such. The problem is the elevation of those things which blind us to the need of God's grace or counting on them for our standing before God. Apart from Christ, your religion is dung, your background is dung, your education and achievements are dung, your work accomplishments are dung, your bank account is dung! When someone comes to Christ they begin where everyone else begins, a sinner in need of God's redeeming grace, and continue as everyone else continues, a saved sinner in need of daily grace.

Paul says, "I have counted as loss" (v. 7) in the past and "I consider everything as loss" (v. 8) now in the present. What you counted loss when you came to Christ you don't try to take back. You continue to count all things as loss in relation to the worth of being in Christ. In verse 9, Paul compares "found in him" with "I have lost everything" (v. 8) because he is now in union with Christ. There is probably a future element in Paul's desire to be found in Christ. He is looking to the day when under divine scrutiny it will become clear that he is in union with Jesus Christ. For that to be true it would have to be on the basis of God's righteousness given to him. This righteousness has been imputed (credited) to us. God considers Christ's righteousness as belonging to the one who trusts in Christ alone for salvation, who now stands before God no longer as guilty but righteous.

When you come to Christ you don't negotiate. You don't offer him anything in exchange for what you receive. You freely receive the righteousness of Christ. We call this "justification by faith," through which God declares you righteous on the basis of the merits of Christ alone. Through the power of the indwelling Spirit "believers confidently wait for the ultimate confirmation of their righteous status before God."[1] Whatever you lose when you come to Christ, you are now found in Christ, united with him forever. Now in union with Christ, you are now united with his people. It is not and can never be "just God and me!" or "I worship God my way."

1. Moo, *Galatians*, 329.

YOU NEED TO EXPERIENCE A DEEPENING RELATIONSHIP AND FELLOWSHIP WITH CHRIST

Paul speaks of wanting to "to know" Christ (v. 10) and resumes the thought of verse 8 which speaks of the "surpassing greatness of knowing Christ." When you initially come to know Christ as Savior you do really come to know him. But it's just the beginning. Our salvation is multi-faceted, like a beautiful diamond. We experience salvation, righteousness by faith (v. 9), sanctification in experiencing the power of Christ's resurrection (v. 10), and glorification at the time of our bodily resurrection (v. 11). This all goes beyond an intellectual understanding of Christ and the gospel. Certainly, the facts are important, and if what the Bible tells us about Christ was not factual then our faith is badly placed. The Bible does not separate doctrine and life. They go together. A greater factual knowledge of who Christ is and what he has accomplished should lead to a greater experience of his presence and power in our lives. Theology should never be separated from a personal walk with Christ. The richness of theology, a greater grasp of the truths of God and his word, should be transformative. If that is not the case, it may be because there is no spiritual life, and theology is merely an academic exercise. You should be in a church where you learn theology and where you hear the great teachings of the Bible. You might be introduced to terms and concepts that are not always easily and immediately fully grasped. You should desire to know more about Christ and live more for Christ. Have you ever said, "There are some things the pastor said that I don't understand?" That's a good thing. Not that pastors shouldn't seek to be clear and understandable or use big words to impress people that many don't understand. But there are great truths that take time to work their way into your lives. And there is nothing wrong with expanding your vocabulary.

In knowing Christ more deeply Paul also wanted to know the "power of his resurrection" and "share his sufferings"(v. 10). This resurrection power and identification with him in suffering are not separate realities but an explanation of what it means to know Christ. Paul wants to know Christ in his experience. We come to experience the power that raised Jesus from the dead. We also come to experience the suffering in different degrees of what it means to live for Christ in a fallen and hostile world. This power is not for self-centered purposes, to become a better "you," or to fulfill your ambitions. You experience the power of the resurrection in your spiritual transformation which does not come without pain, without self-denial, and with a price. Paul wanted to be formed or molded after the manner of

Christ's death, who took on the form of man (2:7). In some sense, which I do not fully understand, there is a reenactment of Christ's death in us as we die to ourselves. We participate in his death at the moment of our conversion when the power of sin is broken. We continue in that participation as we struggle with sin and spiritual disappointments through the power of Christ, that power through which he was raised from the dead. It is the reality that your life is no longer your own. You have been bought with a price, the precious blood of Christ (1 Cor 6:20, 1 Pet 1:19).

Some see the expression "that by any means possible I may attain the resurrection from the dead" (v. 11) as expressing doubt about the manner in which Paul will attain this. Others see it as expressing Paul's humility or that he doesn't know if he will be alive at Christ's coming and transformed, or already dead and resurrected at his coming. We can be sure that there is no doubt on Paul's part about the Savior's power to keep him until the day of final salvation (Phil 1:6). It seems more of a warning against complacency in the Christian life. We should be filled with wonder that God has saved us. We should be filled with humility that God loves us with all the sin and failures that still remain and never believe that his grace and forgiveness are something we deserve. There is a difference between assurance with humility and presumption with arrogance and overconfidence. There is a difference between the sure and solid work of God and our comprehension of it. There is assurance of salvation for the child of God (1 John 5:13). You can know and be sure that nothing can ever separate you from the love of God in Christ Jesus (Rom 8: 38–39). There is, however, a false assurance which needs to be doubted. There are those who have repeated a prayer, been baptized, joined a church, and now believe that they are guaranteed heaven. They think that is the extent of being a Christian, even if there's little evidence of transforming grace, no appetite for the word of God, no real interest in the church, no love for God's people, little change in their pursuits, pleasures, and priorities. Don't be deceived. How tragic that would be! If you claim to be a Christian, then cut and run never to return because you've been disappointed with God or hurt by Christians, then you should have doubts about your relationship with God, and it is a good thing if it leads you to repentance and genuine assurance. The longer you are saved and walk with Christ, and the more you realize the depths of your own depravity, the greater should be the gratitude and wonder in your heart that God saved you. If there's no growth, then the question must be asked if there is truly life.

YOU NEED TO AVOID SPIRITUAL COMPLACENCY OR TRIUMPHALISM

Paul concludes this section with his ambition and our encouragement to "press on toward the goal for the prize of the upward calling of God in Christ Jesus" (v. 14) This upward calling is the target and reward for which believers have been called to salvation in Christ. We haven't crossed the finish line yet. The Christian life is a marathon, not a hundred-yard dash. We are called in verse 13 to forget "what lies behind" and to strain "forward to what lies ahead." During this year, you have had successes and failures. Your successes might delight you to the point where you feel pretty good about where you are in your spiritual life and set you up for a fall. Your failures may discourage you to the point of hopelessness. You ask yourself if it's worth even trying. Paul says, forget them. It's not as if they will never come to mind. Your memory will not be obliterated. But you can't live in the past and allow the past to absorb your attention and impede your progress. You don't have to be a prisoner of the past. We all have a past and have done things we're not proud of and for which we still might feel shame. But for the child of God there's forgiveness and restoration for past failures and present strength for today and the future in your walk with God. Certainly, you don't yet possess all that God has for you. You will not have it all until you see your Savior face to face. Yet there is more than you now know and a greater enjoyment of Christ's power and presence than you have experienced to this point. This is true for all of us no matter how far we have come in the Christian life. Don't forget how far you've come. But in this journey, no matter how far you have come, you still have far to go.

It's a good thing to be reminded that we are not home yet, we have not arrived, and we continue to struggle in a fallen world filled with frustration and opposition. We are on a journey. At the same time, Paul finds great confidence that Christ has made him "his own" (v. 12). The ground of our assurance is not that we hold on to Christ but that he holds on to us. Your salvation does not depend on your progress. But your progress indicates the reality of a genuine work of God in your life. We have not yet obtained the final and full knowledge of Christ, and we are not yet fully conformed to the image of Christ. We look forward to that day. We press on toward that day. If at times you have some doubts about the reality of what God is doing in your life, that might be a good thing. If you are not truly a believer, it indicates that you are concerned and under conviction. If you are a believer, it indicates that you recognize the need for greater effort in your pursuit of doing God's will, where his will grows larger in your life and your will shrinks. Don't be impressed with yourself and your spiritual accomplishments. Don't think you've ever arrived at the point where you can sit back and live on autopilot. We should be glad for every year in which God continues his work in us. There's much to do. We should live with the expectancy that God will continue to do his work in his way in our lives and in his church. We may not delight in all our circumstances, but we can delight in the Lord, that we are in Christ, and that he knows each year from beginning to end. We may be taken by surprise. But he won't. So, by God's grace, better grasp the incomprehensible value of being in Christ, seek to experience a deeper relationship with Christ, and strive to avoid spiritual complacency.

11

Joy to the Nations

Psalm 67

1 May God be gracious to us and bless us
  and make his face to shine upon us, *Selah*
2 that your way may be known on earth,
  your saving power among all nations.
3 Let the peoples praise you, O God;
  let all the peoples praise you!
4 Let the nations be glad and sing for joy,
  for you judge the peoples with equity
  and guide the nations upon earth. *Selah*
5 Let the peoples praise you, O God;
  let all the peoples praise you!
6 The earth has yielded its increase;
  God, our God, shall bless us.
7 God shall bless us;
  let all the ends of the earth fear him!

In 1839, after years of service in Africa, the famous missionary Robert Moffat returned to Scotland to recruit laborers. Arriving at a church one night to speak, Moffat was frustrated that so few people were in attendance and only a few men among them. Moffat had one stirring challenge in his message and those memorable words, with some variations, have been preserved for us: "I have sometimes seen, in the morning sun, the smoke of a thousand villages where no missionary has ever been." In his discouragement Moffat almost failed to notice one young man assisting the organist, a young man deeply moved by the challenge and who responded to the call of God. The following year, David Livingstone, the young man who had heard Robert Moffat's challenge, then heard God's call and sailed to Africa. For the next thirty years he ministered in the interior of Africa in villages where no missionary had ever been. When he died in 1873, his heart was cut out and buried in Africa and his body was sent to England. If you were to visit the tomb of David Livingstone in Westminster Abbey you will find these words inscribed from John 10:16: "Other sheep I have which are not of this fold: them also must I bring, and they shall hear my voice." These are the words which must captivate us today.

There are two main and overlapping thoughts I would like to develop in this chapter. First, God reveals a supreme interest in the nations. Second, God reveals a sovereign intention for his people to make him known through our worship. Above all things, God wants to make himself known and be worshipped. Psalm 67 has been called a prayer for blessing and a summons to praise. It is part of a group of psalms (65–68) called "songs." In this psalm we discover the heart of God for all people, for all people groups. God clearly reveals his purpose—to be known (v. 2), praised (vv. 3, 4, 5), and enjoyed and feared (v. 7) among all the peoples of the earth. God has always been on mission to bring glory to himself and joy to those who trust him through the redemption of individuals from all ethnic groups. He invites us as his people to join him in his purposes. His purpose to be made known must become our passion to make him known.

The psalm builds from the first and last verse toward the center. "May God be gracious to us and bless us" (v. 1) and "God shall bless us; let all the ends of the earth fear him!" (v. 7). Verses 3 and 5 are the refrain—"Let the peoples praise you, O God"—and draw our attention to verse 4, "Let the nations be glad and sing for joy." We see that verse 4 is both the middle verse of this psalm and the central focus, surrounded by the refrain in verses 3 and 5. It is not merely an appeal for hearty singing but an invitation for all peoples to worship, to celebrate with joy and gladness the rule of God. It is our invitation to others to join that great choir of the redeemed in acknowledging the God of heaven who offers salvation to all who respond to his call. There is an anticipation of that day when at the name of Jesus "every knee should bow, in heaven and in earth, and every tongue should confess that Jesus Christ is Lord, to the glory of God the Father" (Phil 2:10–11).

Verse 1 can be translated either as a prayer of petition, "May God be gracious," or as a prayer of thanksgiving, "God has been gracious." Verse 7 can be translated as "May God bless us" or "God shall bless us" or "God blesses us." The fact that the earth regularly yields harvests (v. 6) means we can then confidently ask God to continue his blessing in fruitful harvest. It seems to me that the psalm is most likely a prayer for blessing rather than a thanksgiving psalm, although either can be argued for without altering the message. Psalm 67 "is clearly a missionary psalm, since it looks forward to the rule of God over Jews and Gentiles."[1]

More importantly, we need to ask ourselves a question. When we request God's blessing, or when we acknowledge the reality of his blessing in thanksgiving, what are we seeking, and for whom are we seeking it? God's greatest blessing to us is that he has made himself known. According to Ephesians 1:3, God has "blessed us in Christ with every spiritual blessing in the heavenly places." We should ask for God's blessing while not forgetting that God has already blessed us in Christ. "The blessing of God consists in his ongoing presence in life, his sustaining of the well-being of the world and his [provisions] . . . The shining face of God among his people is a metaphor for his goodwill and blessing" which reveals "a person of good disposition and is a sign of inward pleasure . . . The opposite of God's shining face is his hidden face."[2] Our greatest joy and blessing then becomes making him known.

Verse 1 has a *Selah*, which many believe is a pause or musical interlude. It appears to be used to stop us for a moment before moving on to the next verse. We ask God to be gracious, to bless us, and look favorably upon us, and he does, but why? Before the Psalmist gives us the real purpose of God's favor, we need to reflect on how we might often misunderstand it. While many rightly decry the false prosperity gospel of the health-and-wealth charlatans, it is easy to think that God is primarily interested in our comfort and happiness. The *Selah* leads us to consider God's purpose. God is interested primarily in his glory and in making himself known. God's way is not the American way and at many points counters the narcissistic, self-focused, radically independent, self-satisfied lives many seek. It's easy to fall into the trap of consumerism and reduce God's favor and blessing to material comforts and the acquisition of goods. Certainly, God is concerned about our material needs. He does faithfully provide for his children.

1. VanGemeren, "Psalms," 440.

2. Tate, *Psalms 51–100*, 157.

He has given us freely all things to enjoy. You should enjoy God's material blessings but never let them stand in the way or become objects of desire which deter you from God's purposes. God tells us why he blesses us. Salvation has come! Make it known to the nations! God wants to be glorified among the nations. And nothing should get in the way of accomplishing this purpose, the progress of the gospel, a harvest of souls of which Jesus spoke: "Do you not say, 'There are four months, then comes the harvest'? Look I tell you, lift up your eyes and look at the fields, for they are white for the harvest" (John 4:35).

God's interest in the nations has been displayed from the beginning of time. When God called Abram ("exalted father"), he said in Genesis 12:2–3, "And I will make of you a great nation, and I will bless you and make your name great, so that you will be a blessing. I will bless those who bless you, and him who dishonors you I will curse, and in you all the families of the earth shall be blessed." God changed Abram's name to Abraham ("father of multitudes or of many nations") in Genesis 17:5. He was blessed to be a blessing to the nations through the gift of the Messiah and by faith in him. In the verses before us we find this description—earth (geographical), nations (political entities or clans), and people (ethnic groups with common cultural and social characteristics). These words emphasize the all-encompassing plan of God. There is no one, there is no place, there is no people outside the borders of God's intention to receive worship which he desires and which he deserves. As John Piper writes,

> Missions is not the ultimate goal of the church. Worship is. Missions exists because worship doesn't. Worship is ultimate, not missions, because God is ultimate, not man. When this age is over, and the countless millions of the redeemed fall on their faces before the throne of God, missions will be no more. It is a temporary necessity. But worship endures forever.[3]

The psalm "invites a messianic perspective which looks forward to an age [when God's saving work] will no longer be obscure but will lead peoples of the world to sing of his judgments and guidance."[4] In Moses' time we find this benediction in what is called the Aaronic Benediction in Numbers 6:24–26: "The LORD bless you and keep you; the LORD make his face to shine upon you and be gracious to you; the LORD lift up his countenance upon you and give you peace."

3. Piper, *Let the Nations Be Glad*, 15.
4. Tate, *Psalms 51–100*, 159.

There is something missing in the lives of many of God's people who fail to understand that God did not make known his saving ways or reveal his glory for them alone or for their nation alone. He didn't save you only to deliver you from hell. He didn't save you only to give you an abundant life here on earth. He saved you with a view to the nations, all the nations, all people groups, all ethnicities. This is demonstrated clearly in the purpose for God's blessing on his people in verse 2: "that your way may be known on earth, your saving power among all nations." Blessing in the Bible is often connected to posterity and prosperity. In this psalm we find a petition for an abundant harvest, which provides the image of an even greater harvest—the ingathering of the peoples of the world. "Blessing is [the] bridge that joins worship with the ongoing life of the community outside the place of worship." It is not limited to certain times and events but rather the "quiet, continuous, flowing, and unnoticed worship of God which cannot be captured in moments or dates."[5] When we worship corporately, and as we experience the ongoing blessing of God, we carry that worship outside so that others may worship God in spirit and in truth. God blesses us that we might testify to his greatness and his glory and invite others to join us in praising him. We call for their conversion to bow down before the one true Almighty God, the Father of our Lord Jesus Christ. At the same time we warn them of coming judgment and plead with them to flee the wrath to come. This is our reason for existence. We must not allow anything to influence us and cause us to hesitate in our engagement in the great work of calling people from every nation, from every language, and from every religion to repent and ascribe all glory to the one and only true and living God. "And they sang a new song, saying, 'Worthy are you to take the scroll and to open its seals, for you were slain, and by your blood you ransomed people for God from every tribe and language and people and nation, and you have made them a kingdom and priests to our God, and they shall reign on the earth'" (Rev 5:9–10).

We join in singing the song of the redeemed sung by the two living creatures and the twenty-four elders before the throne of God in the apocalyptic visions of John (Rev 5:9–10). Many take this as an event in the climax of history, and even if so, this is also our song today. Every tribe, language, people, and nation! God's goal will be accomplished as representatives of all nations sing the new song of the Lamb. Declaring God's salvation and singing the song of the redeemed is not for Christians with a special calling. It is

5. Tate, *Psalms 51–100*, 159.

for all Christians, for all those who have been made partakers of the blessing of Abraham and on whose lives the light of the gospel has shone, those to whom the Lord has been gracious and to whom he has given peace. Our hearts should yearn that all may sing the song of the redeemed.

God has made us for this. God has saved us for this purpose. When we confess Jesus as Lord and Savior of our lives, we are then privileged to embrace something greater and more significant than we ever imagined. To confess Christ, to sing this song of the redeemed, is to embrace the peoples for whom Christ died and over whom he desires to rule. Piper captures this thought: "Your heart was made for this, and there will always be a serious or mild sickness in your soul until you embrace this global calling."[6] We should be persuaded that this cause, among all that which is important in our lives, lies at the center of our reason for existence. For many Christians, however, in order to engage in this calling, there must be a reorientation of life and priorities. You won't be able to go on in life with business as usual in following your ambitions. It may simply mean that you begin to think how you and the resources God has given you can be used more effectively for God's purposes expressed in this psalm. It may simply mean that you don't make decisions concerning your work or your place of living based on what you want but based on what best serves God's interests. It may mean that you will never have your dream house or dream job because the Lord has other plans for you to free people from the nightmare of sin and death. You can't pursue the American dream while multitudes live a nightmare of sin and death. You need to be in a place and engaged with people where you can invest for eternity. God's plans may very well at times intersect with your desires. Yet fundamentally we need to seize the truth that God blesses us so we can bless others. God may allow you to earn a six- or seven-figure income in order to live on a lower level than what you could afford and to use this blessing to advance the gospel of Christ. It may mean a smaller house or an older car than what you can afford. We cannot reach the remaining masses of people with the gospel if we succumb to American consumerism and accept the lie that God is most interested in our comfort and enjoyment of material possessions. I know it might sound radical, yet Jesus, "though he was rich, yet for your sake he became poor, so that you by his poverty might become rich" (2 Cor 8:9). Now that you are enriched, you are to make others rich in extending to them the riches of Christ.

6. Piper, "Declare His Glory Among the Nations."

Perhaps there is no more difficult time to demonstrate our commitment to the gospel than in the midst of economic crisis, crippling inflation, and market meltdown. There have been times when many have seen their portfolios sink and their hearts filled with fear. We live with the frustration of the uncertainty of riches, here today and gone tomorrow. Yet we live with the confidence and joy that when we invest in that which is closest to the heart of God, making himself known, that his word will not return empty, but it will accomplish his will, will bring him glory, and truly will be worth it all when we stand in the presence of our Savior with the redeemed from every people, every tongue, and every nation.

Early in his ministry Livingstone said: "Forbid it that we should ever consider the holding of a commission from the King of Kings a sacrifice . . . I am a missionary, heart and soul. God himself had an only Son, and he was a missionary and a physician. A poor, poor imitation I am, or wish to be, but in this service I hope to live. In it I wish to die."[7] Let the nations be glad and sing for joy. Let them join us in singing the song of the redeemed. Let us join God in his purposes and embrace this global calling!

7. Shibley, *Thousand Villages*, 11.

12

Supremacy of Christ in All Things

Colossians 1:15–23

> 15 He is the image of the invisible God, the firstborn of all cre-
> ation. 16 For by him all things were created, in heaven and on
> earth, visible and invisible, whether thrones or dominions or rul-
> ers or authorities—all things were created through him and for
> him. 17 And he is before all things, and in him all things hold to-
> gether. 18 And he is the head of the body, the church. He is the be-
> ginning, the firstborn from the dead, that in everything he might
> be preeminent. 19 For in him all the fullness of God was pleased
> to dwell, 20 and through him to reconcile to himself all things,
> whether on earth or in heaven, making peace by the blood of his
> cross. 21 And you, who once were alienated and hostile in mind,
> doing evil deeds, 22 he has now reconciled in his body of flesh by
> his death, in order to present you holy and blameless and above
> reproach before him, 23 if indeed you continue in the faith, stable
> and steadfast, not shifting from the hope of the gospel that you
> heard, which has been proclaimed in all creation under heaven,
> and of which I, Paul, became a minister.

SOMEONE HAS LIKENED THIS passage to a smorgasbord or all-you-can-eat buffet. You go up and down the aisles to see the selection before you start piling food on your plate. There is so much there you don't know where to start. That's one way of looking at our text. I prefer to look at it as a banquet of fine food, since all-you-can-eat restaurants are not always the best quality. Here we are surrounded by fine food, and at the head of the table we find the host, Jesus. The conversation today at this banquet is about Jesus, God of creation, God of redemption.

The letter to the Colossian church was written during the imprisonment of the apostle Paul. He had received disturbing news (1:8) about the presence of false teaching in the church at Colossae. A system of belief, or, rather, system of unbelief, arose which relegated Christ to a relatively minor place. This heresy, as we call false teaching that undermines Christian belief, was a combination of separate elements—Jewish, pagan, and Christian—to produce something that was novel, exciting, popular, elitist, and required superior knowledge to understand it. This doctrinal error was damnable in that it denied the person and work of Jesus Christ as revealed in the Scriptures, and condemnable as it comes under the judgment of God's word. We live in a time where new, false, spectacular teaching comes to us nonstop. There is a constant stream of new prophets, new prophecies, new promises, new fads, and the latest and greatest recipe for success. You need only follow certain steps, read the right books (even so-called "Christian" books), follow the right blogs, attend the right conferences and seminars, and listen to the right podcasts. We also have celebrity pastors who hang out with the rich and famous, mimic their lifestyles in many ways, in their dress, their mansions, their jewelry, and their cars and planes. They have a veneer of Christianity but in truth deny the gospel.

These verses in Colossians point us to Jesus. We don't need to see everything, we need to see more of him. There are times we can't make sense of life, especially these past few years. In 2020, *Time* magazine's December 14 edition had a front cover with a red "X" declaring 2020 "The Worst Year Ever." If the editors really believe that, it shows how ignorant they are of history. Without much effort I can think of many years with more war, natural catastrophes, terrorism, and atrocities. Of course, that does not diminish the reality of the difficulties faced in 2020, now in 2021, and in the years to come—loved ones lost to the virus, businesses closed, increased mental health issues, increase in drug overdoses, rioting and looting in the streets. We had hoped that 2021 would bring positive changes, but at the time of writing this I am not optimistic. We don't understand what God is doing and he's not doing what we thought he should do or could do. We think we need to understand. God knows that we need more of him. My prayer is that we will see more of Jesus, and seeing more of him we will make more of Jesus. If that is true in your life you won't be unsettled by every change and every event that reminds you that you live in a broken world marred by sin and rebellion against God. There are some things you will never understand. Yet there is a Lord and Savior in whom you can trust. You don't need to pray, "Lord, help me understand." You need to pray, "Lord, help me to see more of you in all your glory, and let me magnify your name."

Paul introduces us to the supremacy of Jesus Christ, to whom you must yield. That is, you must give unreserved and unrivalled allegiance to Jesus Christ. Your allegiance should be unreserved because you are tempted to compartmentalize your life and resist surrendering areas you hold dear and over which you wish to remain in control. Some give God Sunday, but the rest of the week is theirs. Others no longer even do that and have found that the church is not essential to their lives. Your allegiance should be unrivalled because you are always in a battle with yourself and others to serve many masters. You can offer this allegiance as you comprehend the unqualified supremacy of Christ in two areas, creation and redemption, which are connected to his person and his sacrificial work. Why should you offer to Jesus unreserved and unrivalled allegiance?

BECAUSE OF THE SUPREMACY OF CHRIST IN HIS PERSON

Christ is the image of God and firstborn of creation (v. 15). This passage, verses 15–20, may be an ancient hymn. If not, it is clearly set out in poetic form. I don't want to linger on the form except to point out that Paul used a literary form with great beauty to present these magnificent truths—he is the image of the invisible God (vv. 15–16); he indeed is before all things (vv. 17–18a); he is also the head of the body, the church (vv. 18b–20).

The problems faced by these Christians in the first century are similar to our own. There are different words to describe this doctrinal error but what's important are the teachings themselves. According to this false teaching, since matter was evil, God could not have created the world, but he created a series of spirit beings (thrones, dominions, rulers, authorities), each being more distant from him. At the end of the chain was a spirit being which possessed enough deity to create the world but far enough removed from God so that God's perfect purity would not be compromised.

When you fail to receive God's truth about his Son, about salvation, about the world in which we live and the world which is to come, a few things happen. There will be discontentment with reality and the creation of substitutes for reality because people don't like reality the way it is. There will also be a disconnection from reality and the search for alternate realities. These may even be called virtual reality. If you don't like the truth as presented in God's word, then make up another storyline. This perspective presents a fixation on the now, on our present happiness, or feeling good about ourselves. We need more and more innovative ways to keep our attention away from important issues that are ultimate and have a warped focus on things that are temporary, sometimes even trivial. We believe the lie that God exists for our happiness, and since God wants me to be happy, then he understands if I do certain things or live in a way that doesn't honor him or the Bible. The Bible loses its authority and becomes only stories to help guide us in the pursuit of our happiness. Worse, this is often what we see in religion. Religious novelty abounds, but it is not new. What's the latest and greatest? What's working to really build churches? How can we attract people to church with a good show, even add some smoke, or, as one church recently, a beard contest? A church in Pennsylvania a few years ago had a camouflage Sunday inspired by *Duck Dynasty* to attract new members with the start of deer season. This passage helps us regain our focus. It grounds us in the reality of who God is and what he has accomplished for us in Jesus Christ. It is the only sure foundation on which you can build your life with confidence in a sovereign God who sometimes surprises us, sometimes doesn't act when and how we think he should, but who never lets go of us his children.

Jesus is the "the image (icon) of God" (v. 15). Although I can't recall exactly where I read this, I believe it was N. T. Wright who asks us to imagine being in a room separated from another room by a wall with a small doorway connecting the two rooms. There is someone standing in the other room behind the wall. You cannot see that person directly. However, just inside the doorway there is a mirror on the wall. And with the placement of that mirror in the right place you can see the person's reflection. You still do not see the person directly but you have a clear picture. You know who it is, what the person looks like. This analogy helps us understand the relationship of the Father to the Son and how we see the Father through Jesus. Jesus said, "If you had known me, you would have known my Father also" (John 14:7) and "whoever has seen me has seen the Father" (John 14:9). Many people and religions believe there is someone or something out there somewhere. They may give him or her different names but they don't know who or what it is. There is no access to the Father except through Jesus. Jesus reveals the Father. "If Jesus is the Son of God, then he has a fully divine nature. Anything that is true of God is true of Jesus."[1] Any God who is not the Father of Jesus Christ and revealed by him is not the true God. For example, do Muslims and Christians worship the same God? No! The God of Islam is not the Father of Jesus Christ, the eternal Son of God.

To say that Jesus is the firstborn of creation is to say that Jesus holds a position of honor and authority over creation. The Father says, "I will make him the firstborn, the highest of the kings of the earth" (Ps 89:27). Jesus is not a created being. He is the Creator who reigns over all creation. All that exists, he created. All he created exists "for him" (Col 1:16). John Piper observes that you don't stand on the edge of the Grand Canyon to contemplate your own greatness.[2] Rather, you exclaim in wonder that Jesus created all things. All things were created for him, for his glory as the goal of history. In case you're not sure how far his authority extends, we find "all things" twice in verse 16. In addition, thrones, principalities, powers, things visible and invisible, and later in verse 20 "all things" once again. Because it is true that he created all things and he will reconcile all things, he should be preeminent "in everything" (v. 18).

BECAUSE OF THE SUPREMACY OF CHRIST IN HIS WORK OF REDEMPTION

The error taught in Colossae was that something in addition to Jesus was required for salvation. According to false teachers, Jesus wasn't enough. Paul responded by showing the supremacy of Christ as Lord of all. There is a great deal of God-talk today, even an emphasis on spirituality. Around Christmastime each year we hear much talk about Jesus but he is usually kept in his place in a manger. Yet the Lord Jesus, eternal Son of God, is Lord of Creation and Lord of Redemption. Another way of saying this is that he is the Lord of Creation and the Lord of the New Creation. In the first creation, as the firstborn of creation, he created the world and human life and directs human history to its completion. In the second or new creation, as the first-born from the dead in his resurrection, he grants eternal life and will subdue all things, bringing even his enemies to acknowledge to their eternal loss that he is Lord. The Father was pleased to have his fullness dwell in Christ. If the Father's fullness dwells in Jesus, then Jesus is fully God. This is another astounding statement about the deity of Christ. We are to find pleasure in

1. Rhodes, *Man of Sorrows*. 33.
2. Piper, *Don't Waste Your Life*, 34.

the one in whom the Father found pleasure. John Piper exclaims that "God is most glorified in us when we are most satisfied in him."[3] Know who you worship or know who you reject! For some it will be an ultimate triumph. For others it will result in a dreadful experience of judgment.

God has promised that one day all things will be put in their place. We are witnesses daily to the truth that things are not as they should be. We are also reminded that things are not as they will be. Paul uses the word "reconcile" to describe the accomplishment of this goal. The word has the idea of bringing about a change, of bringing all creation into submission and into harmony with God. Jesus will bring everything under his lordship. Every knee will bow, willingly or unwillingly. Has anyone ever told you, "Don't worry. It will be okay"? It may seem trite or inconsiderate when someone says that. You might respond, or at least be thinking, "You have no idea what I'm going through" or "What do you mean by 'okay?'" Will it be okay? You lose a loved one in death, your job, your health, your money in the stock market. Yet in those words people may unknowingly express a truth they don't intend, don't understand, and don't even believe. This passage tells us it will be okay. It doesn't mean you will get your job back, your money back, your kids back, your marriage back, your health back, or your life back the way you want. It won't always seem like it is okay. For believers, it will be. If not now, someday. That's the promise of our text that through Christ all things will be finally reconciled, "whether on earth or in heaven" (v. 20).

The promise is founded on Jesus, who has made "peace by the blood of his cross" (v. 20). Nothing seems to be desired as greatly by most folks as peace today, and in Jesus and Jesus alone we can discover peace, peace with God, trust in him for life and for death, a peace that passes all understanding when you can't figure out what God is doing. As a believer you now know what he has done. And you know what he will do. And you are part of that plan. Imagine! Everything in its place. Creation restored. Enemies defeated. Rebels subdued. Tears wiped away. That longed-for peace finally arrives. Peace! The cry of our hearts. Ever and always sought and never truly found in this world, in this life. This is the promise of the Lord of creation and the Lord of redemption. You've heard the expression when someone makes a promise and says, "You can take it to the bank." Well, you can't always believe it when someone says it. But you can count on these divine promises. Things might not get better for you immediately. But if you are a child of God they will get better ultimately. It is this truth which has

3. Piper, *Desiring God*, 10.

helped Christians endure throughout the ages, suffer loss and persecution, and even their own lives. Consider these verses:

> For you [Christians] had compassion on those in prison, and you joyfully accepted the plundering of your property, since you knew that you yourselves had a better possession and an abiding one. (Heb 10:34).
>
> For [Abraham]was looking forward to the city that has foundations, whose designer and builder is God. (Heb 11:10)
>
> [Moses] considered the reproach of Christ greater wealth than the treasures of Egypt, for he was looking to the reward. (Heb 11:26)

This passage presents the Lord Jesus as the one who made everything, who owns everything, who holds everything together, and who brings all things to completion, all things subdued and in submission to him. There is the promise that every enemy will be defeated and judged and that every believer will finally be vindicated. The error which Paul addresses and corrects is one that wore the mask of Christianity. False teachers did not completely deny Christ, but they did dethrone him. Christ still had a place in the religious system but not the supreme place. Much of what we see in our day retains a Christian façade which makes doctrinal and moral error even more dangerous. Paul sets forth what we need to know in our day—the exalted nature and unmatched glory of Jesus Christ in his supremacy and in his sufficiency. In these verses Paul doesn't tell us to do anything. He will later. Here he lays a solid foundation in setting forth what needs to be our conviction concerning Jesus Christ.

As I said earlier, we live at a time where there is much God-talk and even Jesus-talk which is so far removed from the Bible, with teaching diluted with human wisdom, compromise with false religion, or association with political agendas and social engineering. The God and Jesus of whom many speak are not the ones found in Scripture. If you do not have the Christ presented in this text, you do not have the true Christ. If you have the Mormon Christ, the Jehovah's Witness Christ, or the Christ of liberal Christianity, you do not have the Christ of the Bible. In fact, you have antichrist, of which the Bible warns us and foretold that there would be many (1 John 2:18). If you stand with Christ and for Christ then remember what Jesus said, "If the world hates you, know that it has hated me before it hated you" (John 15:18).

It used to be said that you can't legislate morality. There might be some truth in that, since the problem is with people's hearts that no law can change. Yet we see in our nation today the legislation of immorality. We are no longer talking about tolerance and coexistence in peaceful and civil disagreement. We are now asked to affirm and validate that which God condemns. On a personal level, I really don't care how a person wants to identify, with whom they want to sleep, who they want to marry, or what pronouns they want to use for themselves. They are free to do that in a pluralistic nation like ours. But don't ask me to jump up and down with joy and say how wonderful all these changes are. Don't ask me to cave to the mind police who want to coerce and silence those who stand for biblical values. There are things we as Christians can never affirm. At the same time, we can love people for the gospel's sake and remain faithful to Christ. We must continue to love our neighbor, and we must speak the truth with love and boldness.

As a believer, you know something that many can't see. The one you trusted as Savior is the Creator of the universe. Not only have your sins been forgiven, but you have entered a new world, the kingdom of Christ, and you worship the One who holds all things together which were created for his glory. His resurrection is a guarantee of our resurrection. Today, if you want to know what God is like, look at Jesus. Doing this prevents us from making God into our image. In our minds, we tend to fashion God after our own thoughts and desires. We try to squeeze him into a mold and project onto him something he is not. This good news of the gospel is for you today. As a believer, you can remain confident in God and what he is doing in your life. If you are an unbeliever, he once again calls you to repentance and faith. We have a great Savior! Yes, he came as a baby in a miraculous way through the virgin birth. But he is Lord of the universe. He is worthy of all honor and glory. He is worthy of your worship.

My intention in this chapter was not to beat you up to feel badly about yourself. Neither was it my intention to lift you up so that you feel good about yourself. There are times you will feel both good and bad about yourself in the same day. Today I want you to turn your eyes to Jesus and drink deeply of the bottomless well of his grace, mercy, and love, which are inseparable from who he is: Lord of creation, Lord of redemption, Lord of all. The question for you is this: Is he the Lord of your life? If not, repent today, confess him as Savior and Lord, and begin making much of him in your life.

13

Living in Love and Truth in a World of Hate and Distortion

2 John

1 The elder to the elect lady and her children, whom I love in truth,
and not only I, but also all who know the truth, 2 because of the
truth that abides in us and will be with us forever: 3 Grace, mercy,
and peace will be with us, from God the Father and from Jesus
Christ the Father's Son, in truth and love. 4 I rejoiced greatly to
find some of your children walking in the truth, just as we were
commanded by the Father. 5 And now I ask you, dear lady—not
as though I were writing you a new commandment, but the one
we have had from the beginning—that we love one another. 6 And
this is love, that we walk according to his commandments; this is
the commandment, just as you have heard from the beginning,
so that you should walk in it. 7 For many deceivers have gone
out into the world, those who do not confess the coming of Jesus
Christ in the flesh. Such a one is the deceiver and the antichrist.
8 Watch yourselves, so that you may not lose what we have worked
for, but may win a full reward. 9 Everyone who goes on ahead
and does not abide in the teaching of Christ does not have God.
Whoever abides in the teaching has both the Father and the Son.
10 If anyone comes to you and does not bring this teaching, do
not receive him into your house or give him any greeting, 11 for
whoever greets him takes part in his wicked works. 12 Though I
have much to write to you, I would rather not use paper and ink.

> Instead I hope to come to you and talk face to face, so that our joy may be complete. 13 The children of your elect sister greet you.

MANY OF US GREW up with songs like "All You Need Is Love" and "What the World Needs Now Is Love, Sweet Love." We do need love, but we need the right kind of love. We need love that is clearly defined rather than a love that loves everything without distinction. In our days we hear much more about love than truth. Love has been made to mean many things to many people. Actually, it can be made to mean whatever people want it to mean, and if you don't agree with their version of love than they won't love you. In fact, you might be called a "hater." Truth has become the debased servant of love rather than its partner. Distorted and redefined love is said to conquer all. It even conquers the truth or at least conveniently ignores it. There was a film in 2006 about global warming titled *An Inconvenient Truth*. I never saw the movie because it wasn't convenient for me. I did see a blog entitled "35 Inconvenient Truths" about the movie *An Inconvenient Truth* and a book *The Really Inconvenient Truths*, neither of which I read. The point is simply that there are competing truth claims and not all of them are the truth, the whole truth, and nothing but truth. This is nothing new. People today speak about truth in a way that it can be personalized and adapted to cultural and societal pressures or whatever the latest political agenda requires for reelection. In this respect, our times are little different from the prophet Isaiah's, who proclaimed, "Justice is turned back, and righteousness stands far away; for truth has stumbled in the public squares, and uprightness cannot enter" (59:14). The Bible calls us to love and to truth, to speaking the truth in love (Eph 4:15). As Christians we can experience and express both in understanding the following biblical truths.

TRUE LOVE AND REAL TRUTH ARE MOST GENUINELY EXPRESSED IN THE CHURCH OF JESUS CHRIST

The apostle John addresses the matter of truth and love in this short letter. He wrote three letters toward the end of the first century. Second and 3 John are personal letters written to the "elect lady" (2 John) and Gaius (3 John). John calls himself "the elder," which is probably a reference to both his advanced age and a position of authority. In writing to the "elect lady and her children," this is simply another way of saying "the church and her members." The word "elect" speaks of those who have responded to God's call and have become the people of God. The word "lady" is a respectful term. It's the feminine form of the word "lord" and may hint at the church being the bride of Christ. It shows intimacy and demonstrates the writer's affection for the church and her members.

In his greeting John addresses those who "know the truth." To know the truth means to know and accept the Christian message (i.e., the truth of the gospel). This truth is not merely knowing facts and doctrine, as important as they are. Those who know the truth are brought into a bond of mutual love. Someone has said that acceptance of the truth involves active love. We will see more of that later. Truth leading to love is emphasized by the phase "because of the truth." This truth is in us and "will be with us forever" (v. 2). Truth is immediately accessible and eternally present. Continuing his greeting, John expresses in an unusual way what we often find in letters, "Grace to you and peace from God the Father and our Lord Jesus Christ." Notice how John expands this: "Grace, mercy, and peace will be with us, from God the Father and from Jesus Christ the Father's Son, in truth and love" (v. 3). We are familiar with the terms "grace" and "mercy." God's love and favor are freely lavished on us, and he does not give us what we deserve, which is judgment. God's peace is what we have as a result of grace and mercy. This peace encompasses all the blessings we have in Christ, not only that we are no longer enemies of God, but we are now reconciled to him as friends, blessed beyond comprehension. John differs from other biblical writers in that he positively affirms that these "will" be with us and find their source in the Father and in the Son. To refuse the Son is to cut yourself off from the Father. There is no knowing God the Father apart from knowing God the Son.

TRUE LOVE AND REAL TRUTH ARE INSEPARABLE

Notice how John links truth and love from the very beginning: "whom I love in truth" (v. 1). One without the other leads to the deformation of both. As you may know, there are several words for love in the New Testament. There are other Greek words for love that express affection and seeking one's own enjoyment. There's also the word *eros* (erotic) which is not found in the New Testament. Here John uses the word *agape*, which was often used to express the particular kind of love shown by God to people and must be shown by people to God and to one another. This word is rare in literature outside the New Testament. For Christians, a special word was needed to bring out special elements in Christian love. It is love that gives and that seeks the good of others.

Since love can be counterfeited, John adds "in truth." It might be a way of saying that he truly loves in that his love is genuine. However, it almost surely means more than that. John loves the church in a way that is consistent with God's disclosure of himself and the divine message. It's truth that abides forever. This love in truth is the truth that binds Christians together. When love is absent you can be sure that God's truth has not been accepted. God's truth is inconvenient and unsettling to the natural mind. God's truth is not only inconvenient, but it is also incompatible with the natural, unregenerate mind. Earlier I mentioned how truth has been personalized and individualized. People will tell you that the truth you believe as a Christian is your truth, and they have their truth. It's truth for you. Or others will say there is not really truth at all because truth implies authority, somebody telling someone else to do something. Many want to be their own authority, or at least live in a world of illusion where they try. The only certainty is uncertainty.

I like the analogy of a baseball umpire. The pitch is thrown. Is it a ball or strike? The parameters of ball and strike are pretty well-defined. One umpire says, "I call it like it is." Another says, "I call it like I see it." Another says, "It ain't nothing till I call it." That's not good English, but it is how many look at truth claims today. Truth is what you call truth. It is truth for you. With this view of truth there is no absolute truth, except the absolute truth that there is no absolute truth, no ultimate authority vested in someone or something outside of us. The individual determines truth for him or herself. From a biblical perspective we don't get to play umpire when it comes to truth. God has revealed truth or he hasn't. The testimony of Scripture is that God has revealed truth and that he has spoken through his Son who claimed to be the Way, the Truth, and the Life (John 14:6).

John rejoices to find "some" of the church's members walking (living) in the truth. It may be that not all the church's members were at the time. Or it's more likely that John had personal contact with "some" members of the church when they visited him. "Living in the truth" is the same as "living in the light" or simply living according to God's revelation, the author of truth and the decider of truth, who will judge according to his truth. This is not an option for Christians but is commanded by the Father. Its absence in the life of the church or in the life of a professing Christian is a serious departure from the truth.

It's at this point that John addresses the "dear lady" (church) with two exhortations, "that we love another" (v. 5b) and "that we walk according to [God's] commandments" (v. 6). John has nothing new to tell them on this subject. Jesus had spoken of this command to love as a new commandment, and John would've heard that. Jesus made it clear that others would identify people as his disciples by their love for one another (John 13:35). John writes this epistle perhaps sixty years after the ministry of Christ, and his audience would've been familiar with the command to love one another. The commandments are the outworking of love in its details. Paul tells us in Romans 13 that the commandments "are summed up in this word: 'You shall love your neighbor as yourself'" (v. 9) and that "love is the fulfilling of the law" (v. 10). Love is more than an emotion because you can't command an emotion. Love is active caring for others, participating in their life, and in their joys and sorrows. Love does not avoid being with Christians, indeed, it longs for needed fellowship. The church and its gatherings do not become a convenience, something we do or engage in when nothing else is pressing. It becomes a priority issued from love. It should never need to be coerced. It flows from a heart that has experienced grace and mercy and shows that to others. The command to love can't be fulfilled in isolation or because it's just Jesus and you. He is all you need for salvation, but salvation is the beginning of the Christian life, a journey which leads to the fullness of final salvation in the presence of God. Until that time, God calls us as the church and in the church to love one another. And you can't love others if you avoid them.

As I've already said in another chapter, you may be disappointed at times with the church, with its members, or with its leaders. It's been said that the church is filled with hypocrites. As my dad often said, so is the supermarket, and you still go there to buy food. You won't die from starvation because there are hypocrites at the grocery store. So don't die a slow, spiritual death because you have found hypocrites in church. And when you go there may be one more. Who among us has not been hypocritical? We need each other and we need to love one another, not because we are perfect and never guilty of hypocrisy or other sins and failures. We need each other because we are still deeply flawed in some ways and always will be until the day of Christ. We need to love each other not because we are always loveable, but because God is love, because he has poured his love into our hearts, and because this world really does need to see that Christians love one another.

TRUE LOVE AND REAL TRUTH TOGETHER PROTECT FROM FALSEHOOD AND FROM FALSE TEACHERS

In verse 8 John says, "Watch yourselves." Don't lose what you have gained in Christ by giving your ear, your heart, and your mind to false teaching. There is always loss involved when deviation from truth takes place. In the life of the believer there will be something missing both in life and before God when the "full reward" is not received. John, known as the apostle of love, has strong words for those who deviate from God's revealed truth, revealed supremely in Jesus Christ. In 1 John 4:2 John spoke of those who "confess that Jesus Christ has come in the flesh." In 2 John, these people deny the "coming of Jesus in the flesh" (v. 7). The present tense "coming" is a little surprising. Here the emphasis seems to be on more than the incarnation of Christ, but a denial that Christ still exists in the flesh, that is, a denial of the bodily resurrection. At the time when John wrote this there were false teachers who taught that a heavenly power, the Christ, came upon the human person Jesus at the time of his baptism in the descent of the Spirit, but that the Spirit of Christ departed from him before the crucifixion. So the human Jesus died, but there was no permanent union of the divine Christ with the human Jesus. Let us be clear. There is no salvation in a Jesus who was only human and died only as a human. People who teach anything contrary to the teaching of Christ are considered "antichrist" (v. 7). This word is found here and three times in 1 John. Some use this word to focus on a latter-day antichrist to be revealed in the future before the second coming of Christ and identify the antichrist with the "lawless one" in 2 Thessalonians 2:8 or the beast of Revelation 13. Whoever or whatever that might be in the future, John's emphasis is clearly that this spirit of opposition is already active and has been for almost two thousand years. There may be one future antichrist who embodies all that is evil and opposed to God. However, John's concern here and our concern is the manifestation of antichrists in our day. Those who oppose the true teaching of Christ are enemies of God even if they are somehow superficially associated to what is called Christianity. It doesn't matter how many followers they have, how big the cult or the so-called church, how many celebrities are members, or how influential in the world. And this condemnation comes from the apostle of love. We must never tolerate teaching that cuts out the heart of the Christian faith. We condemn that which stands already under the condemnation of God. We are not talking about different views on subjects which Christians have always debated. We are talking about any teaching that seeks to destroy the foundation of the church, the identity of Jesus Christ, eternal God, one with the Father, from everlasting to everlasting, and coming again in power and glory.

These teachers are described as anyone who "goes on ahead and does not abide in the teaching of Christ" (v. 9). It is speaking of those who offer what they might call advanced or deeper teaching, teaching which goes beyond the bounds of Christian teaching. It might be a claim to new revelation or promising what God has not promised. If you hear someone talking like that, they have gone beyond the simplicity which is in Christ, "in whom are hidden all the treasures of wisdom and knowledge" (Col. 2:3). What should you do when you encounter such people? John tells us not to even "greet" them (v. 10) which has the idea of providing hospitality as people did in that day when there were not places for itinerant teachers to stay. Do not welcome them in a way that provides support for their erroneous and damnable teaching. In our day it also means don't support ministries that have departed from the truth and preach another gospel. It doesn't mean we don't show love and concern for those in error and seek to win them to the truth. But we must not encourage their propaganda and heresy in any way.

In closing, ask yourself if your love for God and his truth has burst forth in a life characterized by living in the truth and demonstrating love to Christians and beyond. Do you love the people of God, as evidenced by your active care and concern for them? Do you love those who are unsaved and care enough for them, for their earthly life finding forgiveness and joy in Christ, and for eternal life in the presence of God that you will lovingly tell them the truth?

I've had people tell me that it's not very loving to tell people that they are sinners and that if they die without Christ they will be lost forever separated from God. If you don't believe God's truth, then don't tell people that. But if you believe God's word you will tell them the truth in love. If you believe what God has said, the most unloving thing you could do is not tell anyone the truth because you don't want to be labeled a fanatic or hater or because you are afraid that you might offend them. God's truth often offends deeply in preparation for a work of grace. Don't be offensive, but let God's word offend on the path to repentance and faith in Christ. Walk in truth and in love! For this command comes from the Father.

14

For His Name's Sake

3 John 1–8

> 1 The elder to the beloved Gaius, whom I love in truth. 2 Beloved,
> I pray that all may go well with you and that you may be in good
> health, as it goes well with your soul. 3 For I rejoiced greatly when
> the brothers came and testified to your truth, as indeed you are
> walking in the truth. 4 I have no greater joy than to hear that my
> children are walking in the truth. 5 Beloved, it is a faithful thing
> you do in all your efforts for these brothers, strangers as they are,
> 6 who testified to your love before the church. You will do well to
> send them on their journey in a manner worthy of God. 7 For they
> have gone out for the sake of the name, accepting nothing from the
> Gentiles. 8 Therefore we ought to support people like these, that
> we may be fellow workers for the truth.

THE GROUND AT GETTYSBURG is soiled by the blood of eight thousand men who died in combat. Tens of thousands were wounded and the battle determined the outcome of the Civil War. There's a sign at the battlefield with the words "silence and respect," which reminds us that this hallowed ground is really a cemetery. Today Gettysburg is visited by both pilgrims and tourists. For some it's a shrine, for others a tourist attraction, surrounded by motels and gift shops, along with a wax museum and miniature golf course. We might forget that soldiers are still buried there, and that people still come to place flowers on graves. In the Gettysburg Address on November 19, 1863, Abraham Lincoln was essentially trying to answer a question. How do you honor your heroes? Lincoln's answer was that no speech you can give, no monument you erect will be worthy of them or of their sacrifice.

A couple hours west of Gettysburg in Somerset County, United Airlines flight #93 crashed on September 11, 2001. The last words of those who died were generally not of those resigned to fate or of people in shock. They were the words of people planning an attack. When the plane crashed, the bodies of those on board disintegrated. There were two hundred fifty pounds of identifiable remains. Some families received a skullcap or a tooth to place in the casket of their loved one. That field has become a cemetery, sacred ground. Again, the question arises. How do we honor them? How do we honor our heroes? The best we can do is remember the cause they died for and finish the job they started.

Our cause as Christians, that of world missions, is greater, more noble than any other cause, and the life-and-death consequences are more dramatic. Piper asserts that the "greatest cause in the world is joyfully rescuing people from hell, meeting their earthly needs, making them glad in God, and doing it with a kind, serious pleasure that makes Christ look like the Treasure he is."[1] Those who take up this cause may never be remembered by earthly monuments with their names inscribed in granite. Their names are written in the Lamb's Book of Life, and not theirs only, but the names of those who were won to their cause. When we come to 3 John, the shortest book in the New Testament (219 words in Greek), we are reading a personal letter that revolves around three individuals. The word "beloved" is used four times (1, 2, 5, 11), and John shows a concern for physical and spiritual health. We find in this text a reference to those who went out for the sake of the name of Jesus (v. 7). How do we remember them? After almost two thousand years we know little of them. There are three men named Gaius in the New Testament, and the one before us was most likely none of them. They are faceless, nameless. We are reminded of what brought many to Christ throughout the centuries in distant lands. Often it was the graves. The graves of those who left loved ones and homeland to tell others of Christ. How can we best remember them? We, most of us who are not frontline missionaries, what can we do? We must continue the work they began in three ways.

1. Piper, *Don't Waste Your Life*, 123.

BY DECLARING OUR COMMITMENT TO THE TRUTH

John rejoiced in speaking of those who "testified to the truth" evident in Gaius's life (v. 3), one of several references to truth in this short epistle (vv. 1, 3, 4, 8, 12). Truth in us causes us to pursue vigorously the way of life indicated by the truth. Truthful living brings great joy, and John finds great joy in Gaius walking according to the truth. Faithfulness to the truth that Gaius demonstrates and that John praises is not merely intellectual assent to a body of beliefs, nor a disembodied commitment to an abstract truth. It is rather wholehearted allegiance to God's truth as manifested in concrete actions to specific individuals. Such a commitment elicits great joy.

BY DEMONSTRATING OUR LOYALTY TO THE PRINCIPLE OF CHRISTIAN LOVE

John goes on to speak about those who "testified to the love" in Gaius's heart (v. 6). We find here commendation for service rendered and encouragement to continue in the days ahead. Gaius is commended for his part in sending out God's servants who went out "for the sake of the name" (v. 7), that is, on behalf of Christ. There are powerful overtones of suffering from John 15:21 in the words of Jesus, "These things will they do unto you for my name's sake." In Acts 5:41 the apostles rejoiced "that they were counted worthy to suffer shame for his name." How many have gone out, have suffered, and have died for his name's sake? A few years ago I read about Muslim attacks on Indonesian Christians which left an estimated eight thousand Indonesians dead in just a two-year period. At least five hundred thousand were driven from their homes. Indonesian Muslims forced as many as five thousand Christians to "convert" to Islam. Christians who refused often were beheaded. As executioners paraded the heads around villages, they struck fear in the hearts of other Christians. During one period of persecution, Muslim extremists torched an average of eleven churches a month for a year and a half. Through the years they burned at least 868 churches, more than in any other country. The gospel often goes forth with a great cost, both for those who preach the gospel and those who accept it. There is no greater encouragement for believers than the fact that what they live and how they die is done "for the sake of the name."

John encourages sending and supporting those who take the gospel to the lost. They are not to accept support from outsiders. They are to be sent in a "manner worthy of God" (v. 6), not only in a way pleasing to him, but as you would do it for God himself. Since they are God's representatives, treat them as you would treat God himself. Believers are to provide financial assistance and support to missionaries of the gospel so they may fulfill the vocation to which God called them. Just as missionaries have gone out "for the sake of the name," so those who support them do so for the glory of that name. John makes it clear that this is not the responsibility of unbelievers but of Christians, "accepting nothing from the Gentiles."

BY DETERMINING OUR PARTICIPATION IN THE TRUTH

Many are content to watch from the sidelines. It reminds me of a coach who described a football game as twenty-four men on the field in need of a rest and fifty thousand in the stands in need of exercise. We are duty-bound to support those who take the gospel to the lost. In doing this, we become (prove to be) fellow-workers. We are not all engaged in front-line activity but equally engaged in the furtherance of the gospel. You become an ally of the truth in disseminating the life-transforming truth of the gospel.

Erwin Lutzer relates a story told by someone who lived in Germany during the Holocaust. The man attended a church which backed up on railroad tracks. As the church gathered Sunday mornings they could hear the train whistle in the distance, and as the train passed they heard the cries of Jews on their way to death camps. The church people were tormented by the screams. When they heard the whistle they would begin to sing, and as the train approached they sang louder to drown out the screams. The man confessed years later that he still hears the train whistle as he sleeps and asks God forgiveness for doing nothing.[2] Can you hear the whistle in the distance today? Will you drown out the cry of those perishing? Will you out of cowardice or a sense of powerlessness do nothing to further the gospel? Will you be content to live as a Christian tourist with your trinkets rather than live as a Christian pilgrim with the truth? Will you be a spectator of the great conflict in the battle for souls, or a participant in the proclamation of the truth? Heaven awaits a decision. There's no middle ground. What will you do for the sake of the precious name of Jesus?

2. Lutzer, *Hitler's Cross*, 99–100.

15

Present Glimpse of Future Glory

Matthew 17:1–13

1 And after six days Jesus took with him Peter and James, and
John his brother, and led them up a high mountain by themselves.
2 And he was transfigured before them, and his face shone like the
sun, and his clothes became white as light. 3 And behold, there
appeared to them Moses and Elijah, talking with him. 4 And Peter
said to Jesus, "Lord, it is good that we are here. If you wish, I will
make three tents here, one for you and one for Moses and one
for Elijah." 5 He was still speaking when, behold, a bright cloud
overshadowed them, and a voice from the cloud said, "This is my
beloved Son, with whom I am well pleased; listen to him." 6 When
the disciples heard this, they fell on their faces and were terrified.
7 But Jesus came and touched them, saying, "Rise, and have no
fear." 8 And when they lifted up their eyes, they saw no one but
Jesus only. 9 And as they were coming down the mountain, Jesus
commanded them, "Tell no one the vision, until the Son of Man is
raised from the dead." 10 And the disciples asked him, "Then why
do the scribes say that first Elijah must come?" 11 He answered,
"Elijah does come, and he will restore all things. 12 But I tell you
that Elijah has already come, and they did not recognize him, but
did to him whatever they pleased. So also the Son of Man will
certainly suffer at their hands." 13 Then the disciples understood
that he was speaking to them of John the Baptist.

Each year after the leaves have fallen, the days are shortened, the outdoor plants have died, and the patio furniture has been put away, we await whatever comes our way. Winter has its charms, I suppose, if only the first snow or maybe a white Christmas. After that many of us begin to long for winter's end and eagerly await the first signs of spring with warmer days, the first hints of flowers and bushes as tiny sprouts appear. We see glimpses that the long winter is about to end and spring in all its radiant beauty lies before us. In this passage Jesus gives three of his disciples a glimpse of his glory which had been veiled in his humanity as something to hold on to in the days ahead when many of them would die for the faith. He gave them hope, not wishful thinking as our English word "hope" sometimes conveys, but confident assurance that whatever happened to him, whatever happened to them, there was a glorious and eternal future.

This event clearly foreshadows the kingly exaltation of Jesus which he recently spoke about to his disciples. According to some commentators this event serves several purposes. It reminded Jesus of his Father's love as he prepared for the cross, strengthened the faith of the three disciples present, justified Peter's recent confession (Matt 16:16), and confirms our confession today that Jesus is the Christ. We confess that although the glory and majesty of Jesus may be hidden and his kingdom unperceived, he is king and is destined to reign as his Father has promised. We now know that "Christ is the guarantee that a whole new cosmos is on its way and has indeed begun."[1] The previous passage in Matthew contrasted the honor one might obtain in human society by concealing one's allegiance to Jesus and his teaching with the shame or repudiation seen in the light of our participation of God's eternal kingdom. Jesus spoke about the self-denial involved in following him. In the parallel passage in Mark 9 he speaks of losing our lives for the "gospel," a reality for most of the apostles, for many first-century Christians, and for Christians in many parts of the world today.

Now Jesus will give us a glimpse through the eyes of three disciples, not only of what will be when he comes in glory, but what and who he is now. Jesus' earlier teaching about denying yourself, taking up your cross, and losing your life for the gospel sounds pessimistic (16:24–28). The disciples needed to see something that would in time enable them to face death, not as an enemy to avoid but as following in the steps of Jesus. We will see that Jesus is more than he appears to be and the same can be said of his kingdom. The veiling of Jesus in his humanity did not alter the reality

1. Rhodes, *Man of Sorrows*, 105.

of his glorious person. Neither does the veiling of God's present reign alter the reality of its present outworking. In the previous chapter, when Jesus spoke of those "tasting death," it was perhaps a reference not only to death but to violent death (Matt 16:28). This event enabled them to see God's sovereignty affirmed and his purposes worked out in the coming of the Messiah. There was a visible alteration of Jesus (our word for metamorphosis). Matthew alone reports that Jesus' face shone like the sun. Luke 9:32 tells us "they saw his glory." That they did not perceive the significance can be seen later in James' and John's request that they be seated in places of honor in the kingdom (Mark 10:35–37) and in the disciples arguing about who would be the greatest (Luke 22:24). All this leaves the disciples bewildered. And Peter didn't know what to say, so he said something about building three tents so the experience could continue.

Moses and Elijah appeared as themselves. We may not know exactly how they looked or what form they took since at the resurrection they along with us will receive glorified bodies. Elijah and Moses were in what we call the "intermediate state." It is the time between our death and the resurrection of the body. We know little about the nature of our existence at that time except that we will be "with the Lord." Why Elijah and Moses? Some see the promise of Elijah's return in Malachi 4:5–6: "Behold, I will send you Elijah the prophet before the great and awesome day of the Lord comes. And he will turn the hearts of fathers to their children and the hearts of children to their fathers, lest I come and strike the land with a decree of utter destruction." A future prophet like Moses was predicted in Deuteronomy 18:15–19. Both these men symbolized the coming of the long-expected messianic age. Both were considered "deathless" in some sense, Elijah taken to heaven in a whirlwind and Moses' grave never found. Both met with God at Mount Sinai and heard his voice. There are even echoes of Exodus 24 where Moses took three men with him before the Lord—Aaron, Nadab, and Abihu. How much of this the disciples grasped we don't know, but Moses' and Elijah's presence evoked a sense of the ongoing purpose of God in the presence of Christ.

You need this glimpse of Christ. You may not sense that you need it today, as life brings few surprises. You will not see Jesus in his glory until you meet him face to face, but you need to understand who he really is, what he began in his first coming when he came meek and lowly to die an atrocious death on a criminal's cross, and what he will do when he comes again in glory and power. There are three reasons why you need to see more of Jesus.

A GREATER VISION OF JESUS PROTECTS YOU FROM THE IDOLATRY OF EXCESSIVE SELF-CONTEMPLATION

In studying this passage I came across a word completely new to me, "omphaloskepsis," which is contemplation of one's navel as an aid to meditation. At the Louvre in Paris there are four large Roman statues of satyrs dating to the second century AD. The statues are standing in a circle looking down and appear to be studying their navels. This is a great image of self-contemplation as an excessive concern with ourselves. Notice I said "excessive." How do we know when our self-contemplation is excessive? In this context it's when the "lose your life" passages seem foreign to you and you yield too much to society, to social media, to the advertising world reminding you of your needs and your self-image, forming your opinions and shaping your convictions. Or when the gospel, apart from your personal experience, seems to occupy little importance compared to your pursuits and ambitions. Our excessive self-contemplation might be manifested in our self-interested pursuits, self-pity, self-seeking pleasure, self-preservation, or any number of ways in which the "self" becomes our primary focus.

One of the great desires of our lives as Christians should be to take pleasure in him in whom the Father finds pleasure and to have the Father find pleasure in us. God the Father loves the Son with the love of delight and pleasure. He is well-pleased with his Son. His soul delights in the Son. When he looks at his Son, he enjoys and cherishes what he sees. When you treasure the Son, you will no longer "make peace with the petty preoccupations of most of American life."[2] What does the Father see in the Son, what does he know about that Son that we might be missing, that we need to know and see? Consider these texts:

> He is the radiance of the glory of God and the exact imprint of his nature, and he upholds the universe by the word of his power. (Heb 1:3).
>
> Though he was in the form of God, he did not count equality with God a thing to be grasped, but made himself nothing, taking the form of a servant, being born in the likeness of men. (Phil 2:6)

So the Son in whom God delights is his own image, reflects his own glory, bears the very stamp of his nature, and is equal with God. Here I want to quote from John Piper again:

2. Piper, *Don't Waste Your Life*, 127.

> Since the Son is the image of God and the reflection of God and the stamp of God and the form of God, equal with God, and indeed is God, therefore God's delight in the Son is delight in himself. Therefore the original, the primal, the deepest, the foundational joy of God is the joy he has in his own perfections as he sees them reflected in his Son. He loves the Son and delights in the Son and takes pleasure in the Son because the Son is God himself. At first this sounds like vanity, and has the feel of conceitedness and smugness and selfishness about it, because that is what it would mean if any of us found our first and deepest joy by looking at ourselves in the mirror. We would be vain and conceited and smug and selfish.[3]

We were created for something infinitely better, nobler, greater, and deeper than self-contemplation—the contemplation and enjoyment of God. Anything less than this would be idolatry. God is the most glorious of all beings. Not to love him and delight in him is a great insult to his worth. It is precisely the pleasure and joy that the Father has in the Son which makes it possible for me, a wicked sinner, to be loved and accepted in the Son, because in his death he took upon himself all the insult, rebellion, and harm that I had done to the Father's glory through my sin.

A GREATER VISION OF JESUS PROVIDES THE AUTHORITATIVE VOICE TO GUIDE YOU IN LIFE

To contemplate Jesus now cannot be separated from listening to him. The Father had already spoken in Matthew 3:16–17 at the baptism of Jesus and proclaimed, "This is my beloved Son, with whom I am well pleased." Now the Father says, "This is my beloved Son, with whom I am well pleased; listen to him" (v. 5). In other words, you and I don't get to live life our way any longer. The Lord Jesus inaugurated his kingdom and although we do not yet see him nor his glory in all its radiant majesty, and although we will never so imitate Christ where the Father finds the same degree of pleasure in us as he found in his Son, yet we will see him in his beauty, and we will be like him when he appears in his glory and his kingdom. Peter recalls this event years later in 2 Peter 2:16–18:

> 16 For we did not follow cleverly devised myths when we made
> known to you the power and coming of our Lord Jesus Christ,
> but we were eyewitnesses of his majesty. 17 For when he received

3. Piper, "The Pleasure of God in His Son."

> honor and glory from God the Father, and the voice was borne to him by the Majestic Glory, "This is my beloved Son, with whom I am well pleased," 18 we ourselves heard this very voice borne from heaven, for we were with him on the holy mountain.

A GREATER VISION OF JESUS PREPARES YOU FOR THE HARDSHIPS AND CHALLENGES OF LIVING FOR CHRIST IN A FALLEN WORLD

Shame now, sacrifice now, losing your life for Christ's sake and for the gospel, is a small price to pay for future honor and vindication. You progressively and purposefully grow in what it means to lose your life for Christ's sake and for the gospel. You understand the futility in trying to have life your way and how much better it is to invest your life rather than squander or forfeit it. This involves the literal loss of earthly life as a potential result of following Jesus. We can extend this to the loss of privilege, reputation, advantages, and comfort. Let us be clear—to cling to life according to that which humanity values most is the sure way to forfeit true life (Mark 8:36). The acceptance of the possibility of death, for the right reasons, is the way to real life. The disciples will learn that Jesus himself in his death and resurrection will soon become the supreme example of this new perspective, one which we cannot adopt without a new and deeper understanding of who Jesus is and a fresh and ongoing experience of his grace.

We will have to ask ourselves this question: Living in a time and place where persecution and martyrdom are unlikely, how should we lose our lives for Christ's sake and the gospel? You may never suffer real persecution or martyrdom for the gospel, but if you adopt the attitude of sacrifice and the investment of your life for the gospel you will be prepared to live for Christ or to die for him. The gospel does not call us to ease, to the advancement of our purposes, the fulfillment of our agendas, and to the attaining of our comfort and material acquisitions. That is not the message we find in the Bible. We must not settle for meeting all our felt needs. We must be about the gospel, about worship, about mission, and about the glory of God. To follow Jesus now in his suffering is to share in his ultimate triumph and glory.

Once again, we need to remind ourselves of Peter's words in 1 Peter 2:9: "You are a chosen race, a royal priesthood, a holy nation, a people for his own possession, that you may proclaim the excellencies of him who called you out of darkness into his marvelous light." By analogy, we realize that much of our way of life and speech was learned from our families, the region of the country or world where we were born or grew up, our neighborhoods. Even our accent gives us away. One time a contractor came to our house in Philly to provide a quote for cement work when I wasn't home. My wife Kathy, a Michigan native, spoke with him, a Philly native. During their conversation he told her, "You're not from here." He knew that by her Midwestern accent. Jesus was not from here. He lived a life that confounded people. Our citizenship is now in heaven from where we look for our Savior. We imitate those whom we admire and esteem highly or whom society considers important as culture changers. We often look back and laugh at old photos and ask ourselves, "What was I thinking?" The more glorious you esteem your Savior to be, the more closely you will identify with him in the way you live and speak. You may confound others who see in you something that can't be explained apart from the grace of God.

At the end of this passage, we find the prophecy concerning Elijah's return has been fulfilled in John the Baptist in his rejection and death (vv. 11–13). This is the pattern which will be fulfilled in Jesus. We see that the Malachi fulfillment as taught correctly by the scribes was fulfilled in a way that was not fully anticipated. The death of Jesus was not the triumph of the opposition but the fulfillment of the divine purpose. The disciples needed to see not only Jesus' destiny but their own. You either live in society which has been called a "vast supermarket of desire" or you will follow Christ with all that entails. Like the disciples, after having a glimpse of the glory, majesty, and splendor of King Jesus, you can never live the same.

You would be mistaken to think that if only you had this experience, then you would have a greater sense of the glory of God. Consider 2 Corinthians 3:18: "And we all, with unveiled face, beholding the glory of the Lord, are being changed into his likeness from one degree of glory to another; for this comes from the Lord who is the Spirit." This text teaches us that one of the ways we are changed progressively into the likeness of Christ is by looking at his glory. We become more and more like the Lord as we fix our gaze on his glory and hold him in view. Although the manner in which the disciples saw Jesus' glory is not what we experience, our experience is not diminished by not seeing something visibly. Hebrews 12:2 tells us to "look to Jesus the founder and perfecter of our faith." In 2 Corinthians 4:4 the apostle Paul describes his own preaching as "the light of the gospel of the glory of Christ, who is the image of God." Two verses later he describes "the light of the knowledge of the glory of God in the face of Jesus Christ"

(2 Cor 4:6). Let us stand in awe of this great God! And let us turn from all the trivial resentments and fleeting pleasures and petty pursuits of life and join God in the gladness he has for his Son.

16

Is the End of the World Near?

Mark 13:1–13

1 And as he came out of the temple, one of his disciples said to him,
"Look, Teacher, what wonderful stones and what wonderful buildings!" 2 And Jesus said to him, "Do you see these great buildings?
There will not be left here one stone upon another that will not be
thrown down." 3 And as he sat on the Mount of Olives opposite the
temple, Peter and James and John and Andrew asked him privately,
4 "Tell us, when will these things be, and what will be the sign when
all these things are about to be accomplished?" 5 And Jesus began
to say to them, "See that no one leads you astray. 6 Many will come
in my name, saying, 'I am he!' and they will lead many astray. 7 And
when you hear of wars and rumors of wars, do not be alarmed. This
must take place, but the end is not yet. 8 For nation will rise against
nation, and kingdom against kingdom. There will be earthquakes
in various places; there will be famines. These are but the beginning
of the birth pains. 9 But be on your guard. For they will deliver you
over to councils, and you will be beaten in synagogues, and you will
stand before governors and kings for my sake, to bear witness before
them. 10 And the gospel must first be proclaimed to all nations.
11 And when they bring you to trial and deliver you over, do not be
anxious beforehand what you are to say, but say whatever is given
you in that hour, for it is not you who speak, but the Holy Spirit.
12 And brother will deliver brother over to death, and the father his
child, and children will rise against parents and have them put to
death. 13 And you will be hated by all for my name's sake. But the
one who endures to the end will be saved.

Almost two thousand years ago Jesus told his disciples that he would leave them, go to prepare a place for them, and return at an unspecified moment (John 14:1–6). When the apostle John closed the book of Revelation from his place of exile on the isle of Patmos, Jesus told him, "Surely I am coming soon." John's response was "Amen, come Lord Jesus!" (Rev 22:20). This has been the prayer and expectation of believers throughout the centuries. As I look around today at the world I suspect that the prayers and expectation of God's people have intensified. It's been long enough now to wonder what Jesus meant by the words, "Surely I am coming soon." We know it didn't mean that Jesus would necessarily return soon according to human calendars and ways of marking the passage of time. Still, we wonder and wait!

In 1918 towards the end of World War 1, a new strain of the flu began making its way across the globe. It became known as the Spanish flu perhaps because Spain, neutral in the conflict with a free press, published the news without censorship. As much as a third of the world's population was affected, with as many as fifty million deaths. After World War 1 both man-made and natural famines occurred throughout the world. From 1914 to 1920 the world experienced seventeen earthquakes. Many saw in all this the fulfillment of Scripture. With the COVID-19 pandemic many began asking again whether this was a sign that the end of the world was near. And of course there are many experts rushing to see how COVID-19 fits into their speculative interpretations. This is nothing new.

In the midst of the pandemic and accompanying panic, my brother John wrote an article to our church asking if COVID-19 was a sign that the end of the world is coming. His answer was a qualified yes. All cataclysmic events, such as the destruction of Jerusalem in 70 AD, referred to in this text, are demonstrations of God's power to intervene in the course of history, and they point to the ultimate destruction of the world that precedes the new creation. However, if by that question we mean, "Is COVID-19 a particular sign that the end of the world is here or near?" the answer is no. No one can answer that question with biblical support. If I could use an analogy, it's like getting old. You wake up in the morning with more pain in more places. Are these pains a sign of your death? Yes, in a sense, since we are reminded with every illness, with every operation, every knee, shoulder, hip replacement, with every hospital visit, that our earthly lives are coming to an end sooner or later. Usually we're hoping for later. Does every new pain mean you will die soon? No, not necessarily, but eventually. You can't escape it. What we see in our world are signs pointing to the end. We don't know when the end will come. Neither should we obsess over it or speculate. Plagues have been part of human existence for all of recorded history. We do well to remember that "if you lived for any stretch of seventy-five years between 1550 and 1720—a big *if*, by the way—you would probably spend one-fifth to one-third of your life under plague-related civil ordinances and restrictions."[1] What we view as "unprecedented" may be true, but only for our lifetime.

Now I need to confess that this passage is controversial, with different points of view and with different interpretations, as with many passages dealing with eschatology (teaching about last things). We are not ignorant of competing interpretations on future events related to Christ's second coming, nor are we indifferent. But in this chapter I'm not trying to resolve those issues. In evangelical circles, among people who take the Bible seriously as the inspired word of God, these views are also connected to the place of Israel in God's program, the timing of the return of Christ, the identity of the antichrist and the great tribulation, and the nature of the millennium. Now, it doesn't hurt to know these views, even take time to study them. That is, study them, but don't insist that you have figured out the details.

In the end, Jesus is coming again. At a time unknown to us, he will defeat his enemies, and he will fully establish his kingdom. All of God's people will arrive at the eternal kingdom, where Jesus reigns forever and ever whether Christ's coming accords with their scenario or not. Are you ready for the coming of Christ? At his coming, will you be with him or judged by him? There is no middle ground here. In answering these questions, you should understand what the Bible teaches and what the Bible doesn't teach. Just as the disciples in the first century, you need to be patient and prepared for Christ's coming and neither deceived nor fearful. Here are a few things to think about when trying to figure out the details of God's future plans.

THE BIBLE IS MORE PREOCCUPIED WITH HOW YOU LIVE THAN WITH MANY OF YOUR QUESTIONS

We are often like children on a road trip. How long before we get there? Are we almost there? Are we there yet? There are many Christians looking for the coming of Christ at the rapture of the church preceding the tribulation,

1. Colman and Rester, *Faith in the Time of Plague*, xxv.

which ignites a series of other events. At the rapture, Christ returns in the air to resurrect those of this age who have died as believers and remove living Christians from the earth to heaven (1 Thess 4:14–16), followed by seven years of the great tribulation (Rev 4–19) on the unbelieving world. After seven years, Jesus returns again at the second coming, defeats his enemies, and establishes a one-thousand-year reign on the earth with Israel restored in the land promised to Abraham. Some believe a new temple will be built in Jerusalem with memorial animal sacrifices. During the thousand years there will be those who do not submit to Christ, born it seems to those who believed during the tribulation and enter the millennium in their physical bodies. Those in non-glorified physical bodies live alongside believers who were raptured or resurrected seven years earlier and who return with Christ at the second coming before the millennium. After the millennium there is a final rebellion and battle which results in the defeat of Satan, who is cast into the Lake of Fire (Rev 20:10).

Other Christians, also looking for what we call the imminent (certain to happen, uncertain when) return of Christ, do not understand Christ's return as taking place in two stages. In this view, and again there are differences, Jesus returns at the second coming to defeat his enemies (2 Thess 1) and to establish his eternal kingdom. Chapters 4–19 in Revelation do not describe a single, seven-year period of tribulation, but describe more generally the course of the present age, and the one thousand years of the millennium, interpreted symbolically, refer either to the present age with Christ reigning over his people or the reign of saints already in heaven. Now that you are thoroughly confused, let's remember something.

In asking questions about the end of the world, as did the disciples, there are some truths that need to be established. Even here Jesus did not directly answer their questions and spoke of events unrelated to the destruction of the temple. For now, let's see that the right questions are not about how and when the world will end but how we will live in a world that does not recognize Jesus as king, in a world that is at war with God, in a nation with elements and movements increasingly antagonistic to Christ and his gospel. Jesus would tell you, "Don't be deceived, don't be alarmed!" In other words, how do you as a Christian live in a world hostile to the cross? Do you cave in, as so many have done? Do you embrace the latest political agenda, right-wing or left-wing, as the solution to our nation's many ills? Are you swayed by arguments for social engineering taking place in our country? Do you find yourself silent on issues where the Bible speaks clearly?

Many Christians and churches are eager to address important current issues, often without reference to what God has said. Fewer Christians are willing to speak hard truths about sin and judgment. There are pulpits around the country where you can attend services for years and never hear about sin or hell, are never commanded to repent, but you will know who you should vote for. Many feel that to speak clearly about Christ and the gospel is unloving, unkind. Let me repeat something you probably heard before and will hear again. If sin will be judged, and it will, if hell is real, and it is, the most loving thing you can do is warn people about the coming judgment and point them to the Savior who was judged in their place. You may not want to speak the truth to people because it might offend them. I think you should rather risk offending people than ignoring their desperate spiritual condition and their need of a Savior.

In this passage, Jesus gives us a glimpse of what lay ahead for the disciples and for those who would follow him, for us his people today. The disciples were impressed with the splendor of the temple. "Look, Teacher, what wonderful stones and what wonderful buildings!" (v. 1). The response of Jesus certainly startled them. Jesus used this occasion to impress on them the temporal nature of human monuments and pointed them in another direction. When you read verses like these in the Gospels or in Revelation, it might be more comforting to imagine that these descriptions of destruction, persecution, hatred, and treachery do not apply to us. But wait, Christians in different places for almost two thousand years have been despised, persecuted, and martyred. It is easy to allow the modern era and world events to determine our questions, perhaps especially in the West. In Matthew's account we find this passage after Jesus said the temple would be left "desolate" (Matt 23:38). In Mark an unnamed disciple asked Jesus to take a look at a temple which the disciple obviously admired for its magnificence, an architectural wonder, even the size of the stones (37' x 12' x 18'). This was Herod's temple, not Solomon's temple, which had been destroyed by the Babylonians centuries earlier. It was an architectural wonder of the Roman world. Jesus' response must have been devastating: "There will not be left here one stone upon another that will not be thrown down" (v. 2). This prophecy was fulfilled in 70 AD when the temple was destroyed by the Romans. The disciples had two questions: When and what? When the disciples ask about "when will these things be" (v. 4), referring to the destruction of the temple, the plural indicates that they understood that other events would be related to this catastrophic event. The request for the sign indicates they were looking to the end of the age and the inauguration of the messianic kingdom. They did not see the long interval between the two events, one local, the other global.

How a Christian should live and die was of far more concern to the community to which Mark wrote this Gospel than the mostly fruitless speculations of our days. How should they live as a persecuted minority which has adopted a new way of seeing and new way living, a way that will lead to martyrdom for many? Much of the speculation concerning current events seems to revolve around an escape mentality. I think this is especially true of those looking for the rapture of the church followed by seven years of the great tribulation. I'm not here to argue for or against this view. This view has many able defenders who do not yield to speculation. When seen in the context of escape, the questions which are often asked and the answers given are far removed from biblical concerns. How often have we heard people announce the end of the world, seeing in present day events some supposed fulfillment of biblical prophecy? Obviously, we should study what the Bible says about future things. But we should not be fixated on figuring everything out; we should avoid fanciful interpretations; we should shun sensationalism, which creates either unrealistic expectations or unnecessary fear.

THOSE FOLLOWING JESUS ARE WARNED ABOUT DECEPTION AND DISTRACTION

Jesus multiplies his warnings about deception (v. 5), fear (v. 7), and the need for vigilance (v. 9). The disciples of Jesus should not be (1) deceived by pretenders or (2) distracted by catastrophic events (7–8). Neither should they (3) allow persecution to destroy their loyalty to him (9–13). We are warned against being led astray by imposters or those claiming some special status in representing God, who promise what God has not promised, who speak on that which God has not spoken. In every age there are false teachers claiming to speak for God, even false messiahs. In our day there are wars and rumors of wars. At the time of writing this chapter there are more than forty active conflicts (Syria, Iraq, Afghanistan, Ethiopia, and many we hear little about). The Council on Foreign Relations lists them in their impact on the United States' interests ("critical," "significant," "limited").[2] These wars and rumors of war characterize the entire age. These things need to happen

2. Council on Foreign Relations, "Global Conflict Tracker."

but are not the end. We must not allow political and social upheaval to upset us to the point where we cannot engage in the work God has called us to do. Disruptions in our society follow from human depravity. These are signs which point to the end of the age, but "the end is not yet" (v. 7). They are signs of the moral condition of our age and point to God's righteous judgment which, although delayed, in grace will not be denied. Second Thessalonians 1:4–10 reminds us that judgment is coming.

> 4 Therefore we ourselves boast about you in the churches of God
> for your steadfastness and faith in all your persecutions and in the
> afflictions that you are enduring. 5 This is evidence of the righteous
> judgment of God, that you may be considered worthy of the king-
> dom of God, for which you are also suffering— 6 since indeed God
> considers it just to repay with affliction those who afflict you, 7 and
> to grant relief to you who are afflicted as well as to us, when the Lord
> Jesus is revealed from heaven with his mighty angels 8 in flaming
> fire, inflicting vengeance on those who do not know God and on
> those who do not obey the gospel of our Lord Jesus. 9 They will suf-
> fer the punishment of eternal destruction, away from the presence
> of the Lord and from the glory of his might, 10 when he comes on
> that day to be glorified in his saints, and to be marveled at among
> all who have believed, because our testimony to you was believed.

We are not merely pessimistic doomsdayers, running around like Chicken Little, trying to stoke fear and create tension and anxiety. We see the world in rebellion against God. We see the vast human conflicts (wars and rumors of wars) and natural disasters (famines and earthquakes) all as signs of an ending world, groaning to be delivered by the coming of Christ and the promised new creation, reminders that this world is our home, for now, but we are pilgrims on a journey to a heavenly city, the New Jerusalem. Jesus said these things "must take place" (v. 7) and are the "beginning of birth pains" (v. 8), like the sharp pains that precede giving birth to a child, painful, intensifying reminders of the coming birth of a new age. In Romans 8 Paul speaks of the creation which "waits with eager longing" (v. 19) to be set free from its bondage to corruption and groans in the pains of childbirth for deliverance (v. 22).

The warning "but be on your guard" (v. 9) points to personal danger. There are perils and catastrophes in the world; there is also the possibility of suffering for our identification with Christ and for the gospel. Christians can expect to be handed over to the authority of the courts. You do realize that what we believe as Christians has been twisted by enemies of the gospel. Christians will be persecuted, Jesus said, "for my sake." Our loyalty to Christ will be tested. God designs these persecutions "to bear witness before them" (v. 9). It is in these terrifying moments that the Spirit will use God's people for effective witness and give the words to speak. Our testimony demands that others investigate the claims of Christ. Rejection of Christ and his claims will witness against them on the final day of judgment. God intends that through this the gospel be preached to all nations. This is good news for those who believe and surrender to Christ's lordship and bad news for those who cry out, "This man will not rule over us!" (Luke 19:14). This gospel has been proclaimed worldwide. There are certainly those in remote locations who do not have access to the gospel. But that number continues to grow smaller. That all nations have had an opportunity to hear the gospel does not mean that every individual has heard. Our responsibility to preach Christ never ends, never changes. Even Paul in his day was able to say that the gospel had been preached throughout the then-known world (Rom 1:8; Col 1:6, 23). Instead of looking for signs of the end of the world we must be busy proclaiming the gospel of the kingdom. Rebels must know that their rebellion will end and judgment will come. They must be invited to repent while there is yet time, before it is too late and the age of God's grace and mercy ends for those who reject him.

Verses 12–13 show the extreme hatred to which Christians might be exposed. Today we are seeing the fanatical hatred of the gospel and attempts to throw off any vestige of Christianity. The text warns that the most intimate family relationships will involve treachery and betrayal. The hatred will be generalized, "hated by all." In these times we are called to endurance, to maintain our loyalty to Jesus Christ. Jesus promises that "the one who endures to the end will be saved" (v. 13). The phrase "to the end" in this verse is not the end of the age, as in verse 7. In verse 13 the phrase refers to the end of one's life in persecution and martyrdom. This is not salvation by works. Our steadfastness does not save us. It is an evidence of the genuineness of our faith which leads to our complete and final salvation when eternal life will be crowned with glorification. As one author says, "Eternal life will consist in beholding the glory of the risen Christ. And eternal life began for you the day you came to know him."[3]

3. Rhodes, *Man of Sorrows*, 113.

THE WORLD AS WE KNOW IT WILL END, BUT THERE IS A NEW HEAVEN AND EARTH WITHOUT END RULED BY OUR GLORIOUS KING JESUS

We understand that the presence of God's kingdom in the world today means that God reigns in and over us, not that we reign. Losing our lives for Christ's sake and the gospel is possible only when we adopt the truth of God reigning in us rather than us reigning in the world. At times in history churches have sought to exercise secular authority over populations. This was true of the Catholic Church for centuries in Europe. It was also true of some of the Protestant denominations after the sixteenth-century Protestant Reformation. It has always resulted in disaster. In our times there may be the temptation to impose our way of life on people, forgetting that our way of life is impossible apart from God's work of regeneration in giving us a new heart, new eyes, and new life. God's political agenda is the kingdom of Christ, presently inaugurated and now awaiting eschatological consummation. All world orders will crumble. All nations, kingdoms, emperors, presidents, Democrat and Republican parties, all will pass away. I believe we live in the greatest nation on earth. I've lived overseas and have travelled widely in countries throughout Asia, Africa, and western and eastern Europe. I've never left these countries wishing I had been born there. It was a gift of God's providence that I was born here in the United States, in Philadelphia, and spent most of my youth in the neighborhood where God saved me in 1973 and where our church now gathers. Our founding documents, the Declaration of Independence, the Constitution, are the envy of many nations. Certainly, our country has not always lived up to these ideals. But as much as I am grateful to be an American citizen, I see nothing in Scripture that ascribes special status or special protection to our nation. We see upheaval and disintegration all around us. As a citizen I'm prepared to fight to protect our freedoms in every legitimate way. I am not prepared to sell my soul for any political agenda. Our first allegiance is to the gospel and to the Christ of the gospel. All else flows from that and is subordinate to that. Everything! Why? Because I believe what God has said in Hebrews 12:25–29:

> 25 See that you do not refuse him who is speaking. For if they
> did not escape when they refused him who warned them on
> earth, much less will we escape if we reject him who warns from
> heaven. 26 At that time his voice shook the earth, but now he
> has promised, "Yet once more I will shake not only the earth but
> also the heavens." 27 This phrase, "Yet once more," indicates the

> removal of things that are shaken—that is, things that have been made—in order that the things that cannot be shaken may remain. 28 Therefore let us be grateful for receiving a kingdom that cannot be shaken, and thus let us offer to God acceptable worship, with reverence and awe, 29 for our God is a consuming fire.

We as the church of Jesus Christ, the people of God, must not pander to a political party—whether right or left, red or blue—or follow any call to action or demand for allegiance which contradicts Scripture or contravenes our calling as disciples of Christ. We may be lonely at times and fewer in number than if we were to follow a populist agenda and jumped on the right bandwagons. I am not suggesting that Christians abandon the political process and abdicate their responsibility as citizens in a modern democracy. I am saying that we must never equate the kingdom of God with any human political agenda. Peter tells us, "You are a chosen race, a royal priesthood, a holy nation, a people for his own possession" (1 Pet 2:9). In Christ, our lives are given eternal significance as we are caught in God's story, as we journey in his history.

There are many voices clamoring for attention today. As a Christian, you don't get to live life your way any longer. You are a subject of Christ's kingdom, part of Christ's church, which does not receive her charter or her orders from the state. There is no political, national, or ethnic allegiance which trumps our allegiance to Christ. Remember that the "political left is not noticeably more interesting than the political right; both sides tend toward solutions that act as if the world has not ended and begun in Jesus."[4] When we witness our world as it is we are reminded that something is wrong and that Someone has come to set things right. The world as it then existed ended in the coming of Christ two thousand years ago! With his conquest over Satan, death, and the tomb, a new age dawned. We rejoice that the "tomb of Christ was the womb of a whole new world."[5] What we see today are the final gasps of a world already defeated and grasping to hold on to power. A biblical perspective should cause us to live well, to enjoy the life that God gave us, to love God and others, keeping in mind that our time is in God's hands and we should be driven to invest well. What good is it if all your dreams are realized, your dream job, your dream spouse, your dream house, your dream vacation, your dream retirement, and at the end you have nothing to show for your life?

4. Hauerwas and Willimon, *Resident Aliens*, 28.

5. Rhodes, *Man of Sorrows*, 105.

The imminent death of Jesus would not be the triumph of Christ's enemies but the fulfillment of the Father's eternal purposes. The disciples needed to begin seeing clearly what lay ahead. They were slow to learn but they came to understand that in light of who Jesus was discipleship could never be the same and neither would they be the same. The entrance of Jesus into the world began something that is unstoppable. Yes, there will be difficult times, persecution, societal upheaval, and chaos. But don't be deceived, fearful, or alarmed. How will you know when the end has come? It's really simple. When God Almighty establishes his eternal kingdom! We wait and we say with the apostle John, "Even so, come Lord Jesus."

So, let's return to the question from the beginning of this chapter. Is the end of the world near? In some sense, the world has already ended. When Christ came the first time, the world as it was ended when he inaugurated his kingdom. When you became a child of God through faith the world as you knew it ended, or should have. When Christ comes again the world as it now is will end. What world do you live in today? You either live in a society and culture where you are encouraged to stand alone, take what the world owes you, and create your own reality and identity. Or you will be part of that band of Jesus followers who identify with him as Lord of all, perhaps insignificant in number, certainly when compared to events which draw huge crowds in our day, or did before COVID-19, mostly for entertainment. You will refuse to exercise power and influence by coercion. You will be like the early disciples, having had a glimpse, faint as it may be, of the troubles which lie ahead and the glory that will follow, but also a glimpse of King Jesus. Bow before him today and confess anew that Jesus Christ is the Lord coming again to reign. May he reign in us and over us today for he will reign forever!

17

Living in the Last Days

2 Timothy 3

1 But understand this, that in the last days there will come times
of difficulty. 2 For people will be lovers of self, lovers of money,
proud, arrogant, abusive, disobedient to their parents, ungrate-
ful, unholy, 3 heartless, unappeasable, slanderous, without self-
control, brutal, not loving good, 4 treacherous, reckless, swollen
with conceit, lovers of pleasure rather than lovers of God, 5 having
the appearance of godliness, but denying its power. Avoid such
people. 6 For among them are those who creep into households
and capture weak women, burdened with sins and led astray by
various passions, 7 always learning and never able to arrive at a
knowledge of the truth. 8 Just as Jannes and Jambres opposed Moses, so these men also oppose the truth, men corrupted in mind
and disqualified regarding the faith. 9 But they will not get very
far, for their folly will be plain to all, as was that of those two men.
10 You, however, have followed my teaching, my conduct, my aim
in life, my faith, my patience, my love, my steadfastness, 11 my
persecutions and sufferings that happened to me at Antioch, at
Iconium, and at Lystra—which persecutions I endured; yet from
them all the Lord rescued me. 12 Indeed, all who desire to live a
godly life in Christ Jesus will be persecuted, 13 while evil people
and impostors will go on from bad to worse, deceiving and being
deceived. 14 But as for you, continue in what you have learned and
have firmly believed, knowing from whom you learned it 15 and
how from childhood you have been acquainted with the sacred
writings, which are able to make you wise for salvation through

> faith in Christ Jesus. 16 All Scripture is breathed out by God and profitable for teaching, for reproof, for correction, and for training in righteousness, 17 that the man of God may be complete, equipped for every good work.

WHAT DO WE NEED to know and do in reference to the last days? We saw in an earlier chapter that in Christian circles there is an enormous amount of speculation about the last days. Are we in them? Are there signs indicating that Jesus is returning soon? Are there historical events that will trigger Christ's return? I remember seeing an old friend whom I hadn't seen for fifteen or twenty years. After our greeting he immediately launched into a monologue on current events in the Mideast and how things were coming together which signaled that Jesus must be coming back soon. These speculations often lead to scams that present current events as a reason to invest in something that in the end only benefits the scammers. I think of the Iraqi dinar scam, targeting those who believed they would make millions by buying cheap Iraqi dinars, awaiting an increase in value of the dinar by a hundred times or more. They are still waiting.

The apostle Paul writes during a time of imprisonment in Rome knowing he will not be released. His words are the words of a man soon to die. He does not offer speculation. He offers substance—warnings, encouragements, and promises that depend on the faithfulness of God and God's word. I'm not suggesting that we should not live with expectancy, especially the expectancy of the imminent return of Christ. Yet rather than speculating on the timing of Christ's return, the apostle Paul would point us to the sufficiency of Christ and the sufficiency of Scripture to lead godly lives in these last days. We live in a world described by Blaise Pascal almost four hundred years go: "Since man has lost the true good, everything can appear equally good to him, even his own destruction, though so opposed to God, to reason, and to the whole course of nature."[1] We are living in the last days. We are living in evil times. We can debate whether these times are more evil than in the past. We certainly have more media access to evil around the globe and the technological capacity for greater acts of evil and destruction. Yet the evil which finds its source in the evil human heart has been with us since the beginning of time, with the first murder by Cain of his brother Abel. Yes, the last days are a time of unbridled evil. Yet we as God's people have the high calling to live in these times as light bearers as we call others

1. Pascal, *Pensées*, 114.

to the marvelous grace and light found in Jesus Christ. To live in these last days in honoring our calling as God's people, there are three challenges that you need to take seriously.

YOU MUST UNDERSTAND THE TIMES IN WHICH YOU LIVE

We begin to understand our times by looking at the times in which the disciples lived. In these verses we have a general picture with some local color of the evil associated with the "last days." This letter was written to Timothy as a young pastor with application for all believers. The prophecy of the last days has immediate reference to the local situation and specific examples of their present circumstances with principles for our benefit. As always, Paul points to the sufficiency of Christ and the Scriptures in every age. We live in the last days, as did those who were alive in the first century (Acts 2:17; Heb 1:2). The last days are the present age of the Spirit launched by Jesus' death, burial, and resurrection and which culminate in God's final intervention at the second coming of Christ to perfect our salvation and execute judgment on the ungodly.

Keep in mind that when Paul speaks of "people" this is not a general reference to sinners but a specific reference to those who have abandoned the truth. Paul employs a "vice-list" technique to establish deviance from the values that produce virtue with a focus on evil and danger. He employs seventeen adjectives and two contrasts in no particular order and brackets this section by two kinds of misguided love: self-love (v. 2) and love of pleasure (v. 4). The first four descriptors are broad—self-centeredness, immoral tendencies from basic selfish disposition, wrong attitudes and sinful behavior toward others, and deficiencies of character. Verse 2 speaks of someone "abusive" (slanderer), "disobedient to parents" (rebellious). Verse 3 describes the "heartless" (without love) and "unappeasable" (unforgiving), this last word used only here in the New Testament. The word "unappeasable" describes an attitude that refuses reconciliation and leads to the destruction of relationships and lives. These people are portrayed as "lacking self-control" (restraint) and "brutal," a word which typically describes wild animals and those that behave like them. Verse 4 continues with a depiction of "lovers of pleasure rather than lovers of God," where pleasure comes first in inclination. This list is different from the list of sins in Romans 1:29–32. The behavior in Romans describes unbelievers who have never acknowledged God.

Second Timothy 3 describes professing believers who have defected from the faith. In verse 5 we find a transition from general prophecy to the actual situation. These people have a "form of godliness" characterized by pretense and lack of substance, but "denying (lacking) its power," that is, the role of the Holy Spirit in enabling Christian living, service, and suffering. They possess a superficial piety or pretense and are cloaked in religious garb. They claim to know God but deny him with their works (Titus 1:16), possessing a counterfeit spirituality that is empty of the Spirit's indwelling presence.

YOU MUST AVOID FALSE TEACHERS

Paul warns true believers about those who have an outward appearance of piety but lacked reality. They use religious jargon but deny God's moral claims. Paul says, "Continue to turn away from them!" This call for separation may mean exclusion or expulsion from the church. Compare the redemptive approach found in 2 Timothy 2:23 toward those in error. These false teachers are now hardened in their opposition. They are described as deceitful ("worm their way in") and ruthless in their dominance over victims. These victims were especially women in Ephesus who lacked spiritual insight and were targets for smooth, smarmy, false teachers. Paul is not making a general statement about women and certainly did not have a low opinion of women. He's speaking about a specific group of women who were seen as easy prey for the predators. These women were vulnerable and victimized, burdened by past sins in their consciences and dabbling in religious novelties. Their situation was similar to those today who are targeted by false teachers who promise prosperity to the impoverished and health to the sick, usually requiring a monetary donation, making promises the Bible does not make, and in the end producing casualties. They present a caricature of Christianity and bring reproach on Christ's name. We see in verses 8–9 that these opponents to the truth are hardened apostates who have been exposed to the truth. They rejected the truth, all the while claiming to be Christians. They redefined the true gospel, which they considered insufficient or uncomfortable. They remade the gospel into something more accommodating for their audience. Later in this letter Paul describes the audience as people who "will not endure sound teaching, but having itching ears they will accumulate for themselves teachers to suit their own passions, and they will turn away from listening to the truth and wander off into myths" (4:3–4). The false teachers in reality are pagans with "depraved minds" in opposition to God.

Paul draws on events connected with Moses' leadership and those who opposed him. The faith of false teachers was reckoned worthless and rejected, and their efforts to oppose the truth would ultimately fail. They would not succeed because "their folly will be plain to all" (v. 9). God's people would triumph over the opposition. As an aside, perhaps we might see some present application in the political circuses of our day where some candidates try to outdo others in their claim to be "Christian." Whether they actually are Christians, God knows. But it often seems like the claim is more about attracting votes than a reality. And to end speeches with "God bless America" often sounds hollow and disingenuous. We must resist the temptation to mold the gospel to the point where we feel comfortable, unchallenged, where the gospel has been tamed to the point that it loses its teeth, its convicting power in our lives, and where we sit in judgment over the gospel and conform it to our expectations rather than allowing it to conform us to the image of Christ. Going back to the vice list of verses 2–5 it becomes obvious that these are sins to which we all are susceptible. In this sense the list of sins becomes not simply a portrait of "them" versus "us" but also a mirror that reflects tendencies in our own character with the potential to become lazy, uncommitted believers. Following the gospel as Paul did might then actually lead to the persecution which Paul experienced and which he says will be true in some way for "all who desire to live a godly life in Christ Jesus" (v. 12). In other words, if we never pay any price for what we believe, we have to ask ourselves questions about its value. In applying this passage to our own lives, we should understand that character determines behavior, although we can adjust our behavior temporarily to correspond to what is socially or religiously expected and acceptable. This leaves us with the challenge of allowing God to mold and alter our character. The love of self produces all kinds of evil and points to our need for God to keep us from being filled with folly and unbelief.

YOU MUST CONTINUE IN REVEALED TRUTH

Paul draws out lessons from his life for the benefit of young Timothy, including hardships related to preaching the gospel. Notice the contrast between the vice list in verse 2–5 and the list of nine virtues and experiences which characterized his ministry, including "persecutions and sufferings"

(vv. 10–11). Godly followers of Christ should expect to suffer at some point in life. This persecution "may vary in degree and take different forms but the basic hostility of the world to the godly man remains unchanged."[2] Evil imposters who progress only in the direction of evil and bondage lose the ability to distinguish between truth and falsehood. The combined impact of godly teachers and inspired Scripture promotes endurance in our lives just as it did for Timothy. There is no need to search out novelties on which to squander your energy. You need to sit under a sound ministry and remain in the truths you have learned. Scripture points to the Savior who provides salvation, and the profitability of Scripture lies in its inspired character. Scripture is God-breathed; it has its origin in God (v. 16). God speaks to us and transforms us by his word, the source of Christian doctrine ("teaching"), which exposes errors in false teaching and reproof in our personal lives ("rebuking"), restores us to a right state before God ("correcting"), and leads to righteous living, to a holy lifestyle ("training"). You should avoid anyone who claims a special connection with God and has God speaking to them apart from Scripture. Beware of anyone who says, "God told me."

We can look at the lives of faithful Christians in the past and present to see the faithfulness of God amid hardship and the need for perseverance. God's sufficient word equips us to be fully qualified and prepared to undertake whatever tasks God puts before us. Understand the times in which you live. Don't follow speculation and false teaching. While novel teaching may be captivating, entertaining, and self-satisfying, it is ultimately under the judgment of God. Continue in the truth of the gospel, its power to not only save you from sin and judgment but also to continually transform your life and protect you from destructive error.

2. Hiebert, *Second Timothy*, 94.

18

Faithful Living in Times of Struggle

Nehemiah 2:17–20

> 17 Then I said to them, "You see the trouble we are in, how Jeru-
> salem lies in ruins with its gates burned. Come, let us build the
> wall of Jerusalem, that we may no longer suffer derision." 18 And
> I told them of the hand of my God that had been upon me for
> good, and also of the words that the king had spoken to me. And
> they said, "Let us rise up and build." So they strengthened their
> hands for the good work. 19 But when Sanballat the Horonite and
> Tobiah the Ammonite servant and Geshem the Arab heard of it,
> they jeered at us and despised us and said, "What is this thing that
> you are doing? Are you rebelling against the king?" 20 Then I re-
> plied to them, "The God of heaven will make us prosper, and we
> his servants will arise and build, but you have no portion or right
> or claim in Jerusalem."

After the Exile to Babylon in 586 BC, God allowed his people to return to the land around 538 BC during the reign of King Cyrus the Persian and under the leadership of Zerubbabel and Joshua. The work on the Temple was begun, then halted until 520, when under the preaching of the prophet Haggai the work began again and the temple was completed in 516 BC. More than half a century later Ezra led another return in 458 BC when the Jewish community was struggling to maintain its identity and was insecure due to the severe moral and religious challenges presented by the need to remain a faithful and distinctive people. You see already the parallels with the times in which we live. In that time and in these times we see the faithfulness of God in rescuing and restoring his people in the face of, humanly speaking, insurmountable odds. We are reminded that the covenant community, both then and now, is prone to failure in its calling as a faithful people. We need a greater understanding of our place in God's community and to recognize how our worship demonstrates the reality of our confession as members of the believing community, the church of Jesus Christ. After the ministry of Ezra, Nehemiah, who served in the court of King Artaxerxes, arrived in Jerusalem in 445 BC and found the walls broken down, the city defenseless against its enemies, and the people demoralized. The people needed not only a man of God to lead them, but the God of heaven to empower them and restore them to a place of confidence in their God and to give them a heart to serve him in the midst of struggles and opposition. The people needed hope that was well placed.

There were ten gates in Jerusalem at this time, starting from the Sheep Gate on the north edge of the city. In Nehemiah 2:13 Nehemiah inspects the Dung Gate. Chapter 3 lists the gates and the workers rebuilding the wall. This work was not without some resistance. Certain "nobles would not stoop to serve their Lord" (3:5). They didn't want to get their hands dirty. In 3:14 we come to the Dung Gate. Who gets to work there? Now if I was supervising, it would probably be someone other than me. Logically I think Hananiah, one of the perfumers, would be the ideal candidate. But it was Malchijah, son of Rechab, who was given the task. Perhaps he was a Rechabite, a descendant of Jehonadab who forbade his descendants to drink wine or to live in cities (Jer 35:14). If so, there's irony in the name of the district where Malchijah was ruler—Beth-haccherem, or house of wine.

This story reminds me of the time my wife and I were living outside Paris, France, a few years ago. The town where we lived had scooter vacuums with a hose. When we went out for a walk we could hear the scooters coming and smell them going. The scooters were not there to clean up trash but dog droppings, since many French seemed reluctant to pick up after their dogs with a doggy sack. Now I don't know what it smelled like at the Dung Gate and don't want to exaggerate the special challenges of working there. Of course I would like to ask Hanun why he and the others repaired five hundred yards of wall but stopped at the Dung Gate (v. 13). Most likely it was named Dung Gate since it was the gate closest to the garbage dump outside the walls of Jerusalem.

This story leads me to ask a question. How is it going with you in your life? You may feel stuck where you are. You might be saying that you can't stand what you do every day. Some things you are doing may seem useless, menial, or trivial in the short term. You may not be appreciated. You may hate your job at times but love the people you work with or vice versa. They may hate their job as well but as a Christian your work has a value that cannot be measured in a paycheck, promotions, or titles. There are several principles I draw from this passage.

THE IMPORTANCE OF YOUR LIFE CANNOT BE MEASURED BY OUTWARD CIRCUMSTANCES

My family lived in France for several years, and we were amazed at the architectural gems we encountered throughout the country. Imagine the opportunity to visit the Paris Opera and Paris sewers, which were both open for visits. Which would you rather visit? Which is more attractive? Which is more important? The sewers could exist without the Opera. The Opera could exist without the sewers, but only for one performance. You see, nothing great as determined by God gets accomplished without someone working behind the scenes. For example, I drink coffee every morning. I did not plow the ground. I did not plant the seeds. I did not pull the weeds. I did not pick the beans, pack them, ship them, sell them. I didn't even grind them. I bought them in a bag and put them in a coffee maker. Which job along the way is the most important? Some are harder than others. Some require more skill than others. Some pay better than others. So wherever you find yourself along the way in life's journey, do what you do for the Lord. And if you cannot do it for the Lord, then maybe it is time to find something else to do. Consider Jeremiah 45:5: "And do you seek great things for yourself? Seek them not!" Great personal success and the fulfillment of your ambitions is not always what God has planned for you. Václav Havel was the last president of Czechoslovakia and first president of the Czech Republic. He said that "the real test of a man is not when he plays the role that he wants for himself but when he plays the role destiny has for him." You may never be in the spotlight and don't need to be.

Let's look at Nehemiah's life. Initially, God seems to prosper Nehemiah. He rose through the ranks of Artaxerxes's court to the prestigious and highly trusted position of the king's cupbearer (1:11). This provided him close proximity to and high credibility with the king. This in turn caused the king to notice Nehemiah's sadness over Jerusalem and desire to do something about it (2:2). Soon Nehemiah was off to Jerusalem with a royal leave of absence, building permit, and military escort. When he arrived he quickly mobilized volunteers to rebuild sections of the city's crumbled wall. And these folks "had a mind to work" (4:6). Things were going very well until Sanballat and Tobiah entered the picture (4:7). Their people remembered Judah's former regional dominance. A rebuilt Jerusalem meant a Jewish resurrection, and they were determined to keep the tomb closed. They tried everything. They jeered, insulted, threatened attack, plotted assassinations, and intimidated Jewish families. They even threatened to tell Artaxerxes that his cupbearer had treasonous plans to appoint himself king of Judah (6:7). But none of this worked. The "good hand of God" (2:8), evident from the beginning of the undertaking, remained on Nehemiah as his hands were strengthened (6:9).

The enemies did, however, slow the progress. Half of the crew stopped building in order to stand guard and the other half worked while carrying weapons (4:21). Even at night they remained battle-ready (4:22). This was a costly distraction. Productivity would have more than doubled with focused, rested workers. God had given Nehemiah favor with mighty Artaxerxes. He could have done the same with Sanballat and Tobiah. Why did God allow so much wasted time, energy, and money? The truth is, he didn't. In God's economy none of these resources were wasted. They were invested in building something far more important and precious than a wall. God was building faith. A rebuilt city and a faithless people would not please God (Heb 11:6). So, as Nehemiah and the people worked to rebuild Jerusalem, God worked through opposition to build their dependent faith in his power rather than their own. It was the opposition that prompted Nehemiah to preach, "Do not be afraid of them. Remember the Lord, who is great and awesome, and fight for your brothers, your sons, your daughters, your wives, and your homes" (4:14).

THERE IS A UNIQUENESS WITH WHICH EACH CHRISTIAN HAS BEEN ENDOWED BY GOD

Where you work and live may not always be pleasant, but real pleasure is derived from seeing God at work in and through you. When our family entered Romania in 1994, medical care was not nearly at the level of care we had received in France. I still vividly remember carrying our youngest son crying from the doctor's office after he was given penicillin shots in the leg because no other antibiotics were available. Sometimes God calls you to a harder place. And if you are accustomed to ease and immediacy in getting things done, it becomes more difficult to adjust to new challenges. Listen, you may never have the position in life you think you deserve or that you think your gifts merit, but you can learn to serve God where he has placed you with great satisfaction and great reward. You may also experience opposition, as Nehemiah did, and wonder why. God brings much into our lives we would not ask for, but he knows it is what we need. I am thankful that God is at work in placing people in strategic places for his harvest. I am thankful for those who do not leave challenging places without clear direction from the Lord in order to seek greener pastures. I am thankful for those whom God has found or placed in circumstances that others may envy, and yet they have a heart for God's work and make great sacrifices to serve God. What is important is finding the place God has for you and not the place others think you should be. Ask yourself, have you found your place at this time, at this stage of your life, in the work and the purposes of God, or do you remain fixated on what you want in life and consider what God wants only if it suits you?

IN CHRIST AND THE GOSPEL YOU FIND A NEW IDENTITY

You can find a measure of fulfillment in what you are doing as a job. There is nothing wrong with being happy on your job and loving your work. But do not let it be your identity. How often we have seen people come to Christ, or immigrants come to the United States, who begin faithfully attending worship services on Sunday until they have an opportunity to make more money. Then they disappear. Thankfully that's not true of all new believers or immigrants. When you understand who you are in Christ, what God has done for and in you through the gospel, you begin to see the importance of pursuing faithfulness in the task to which God has called you and which contributes to the work of God. Every Christian should ask at times, "How does what I am doing fit into God's purposes?" Is it even a consideration in your decisions? Most of us will remain obscure in the eyes of others, but you are precious in the Lord's eyes.

The truth is that you may never climb many rungs on that ladder of success if you live a life of obedience under the sway of God's word. You will find more and more that your Christian convictions may be enough to bring opposition to your plans to advance your career. If you fail to understand that truth, you will rarely find joy in the journey because you will focus on apparent failures that hinder you in accomplishing your dreams. You will live from disappointment to disappointment and wind up bitter at God and others because life did not turn out the way you thought it would. You may chase dreams that are your own, which become nightmares. "Lord, help me to be content with you, and serve you where you have placed me." You may not always know what the Lord is doing in your life. But he does! Wait on him. Be faithful today and tomorrow. And you will find him faithful.

19

Forgiven and Restored: Time to Follow Jesus!

John 21:15–19

> 15 When they had finished breakfast, Jesus said to Simon Peter,
> "Simon, son of John, do you love me more than these?" He said to
> him, "Yes, Lord; you know that I love you." He said to him, "Feed
> my lambs." 16 He said to him a second time, "Simon, son of John,
> do you love me?" He said to him, "Yes, Lord; you know that I love
> you." He said to him, "Tend my sheep." 17 He said to him the third
> time, "Simon, son of John, do you love me?" Peter was grieved be-
> cause he said to him the third time, "Do you love me?" and he said
> to him, "Lord, you know everything; you know that I love you." Je-
> sus said to him, "Feed my sheep. 18 Truly, truly, I say to you, when
> you were young, you used to dress yourself and walk wherever you
> wanted, but when you are old, you will stretch out your hands, and
> another will dress you and carry you where you do not want to go."
> 19 (This he said to show by what kind of death he was to glorify
> God.) And after saying this he said to him, "Follow me."

When I was a child my brothers and I sometimes dreaded my father returning home from work. My mother had put up with our bad behavior and disobedience all day but often waited for our dad to come home for the discipline, which was often a spanking we deserved. My mom would say, "Wait until your father comes home." We did wait and we worried about what would happen, what story we would tell, when it came time to face our dad. On a much greater scale, imagine Peter waiting to meet the Savior he denied three times. It has been a week since the resurrection. Jesus had appeared to the disciples as a group. Now he was going to meet Peter. Peter needed to be confronted about his denial, especially since he had been so bold and announced that if everyone abandoned Jesus, he would never abandon him (Matt 26:33). Jesus is coming to meet Peter. The moment of reckoning has arrived.

The story opens with several of the disciples back in Galilee. This was the third appearance of Jesus to his disciples (v. 14). They were fishermen by trade but spent a night without success. At the word of Christ they let down their nets and brought in 153 fish (v. 11). This account also informs us about the nature of the resurrection which we await, because the Bible tells us that we will be like Christ, transformed with a new body but with our identity preserved and with some kind of material existence. Jesus prepared a fire and breakfast and ate with his disciples (v. 12). Certainly he did not need to eat but did eat after his resurrection. Jesus had told them they would be fishers of men. After the crucifixion they had returned to their previous occupation. We shouldn't be too hard on them. They were still confused about what had taken place and they needed to put food on the table. Peter has some lessons to learn. One of them is that he, in spite of his boasting, cannot be the man he wants to be or the man that God wants him to be in his own strength. It's a lesson we all must learn if we are to faithfully serve God. Notice the setting—a charcoal fire made by a friend (v. 9). Perhaps a reminder that Peter had warmed himself at a fire made by Christ's enemies (18:18). These are the only places this word for "charcoal fire" is used in the New Testament. We see Peter as a man ravaged by guilt. He will be restored by grace. He will respond in gratitude. Keep those three thoughts in mind. They are foundational for the Christian life. Here are three applications I find in this passage.

DON'T BOAST OF WHAT YOU WILL DO FOR CHRIST, BUT BOAST IN WHAT HE HAS DONE FOR YOU

There's really no place for boasting in the Christian life. When we are honest about what we were, what God saved us from, and honest about our own weaknesses, we can stop pretending that we are what we are, have what we have, and have accomplished what we've done because of our intelligence, our wisdom, and strength. My mom used to say to her boastful, big-mouthed teenage sons, "Self-praise stinks." It might seem harsh to hear Jesus question Peter three times. But keep in mind that Peter denied Christ three times and had boasted that he would follow Christ to the death (John 13:36–38; Matt 26:30–35). For me, one of the saddest and most touching passages in the Bible is found in Luke 22:61–62, "And the Lord turned and looked at Peter. And Peter remembered the saying of the Lord . . . And he went out and wept bitterly."

Peter had held a privileged position in the inner circle of Jesus, had been prepared for responsible leadership, and needed to be reestablished in line with the seriousness of his defection. Peter was now under a cloud with his fellow disciples after the denial. He had denied all connection with the Lord in the presence of the enemy. Now he is called upon to affirm his love for the Lord in the presence of friends. Three times Jesus asked the question. The first time: "Do you love me more than these?" (v. 15). The word "these" could mean: 1) More than these men love me; 2) more than these things; or 3) more than you love them? Twice Peter answers, "Yes, Lord, you know that I love you" (vv. 15, 16). Peter does not attempt to answer in relation to his friends, but he appeals to the Lord's knowledge that he truly loves him, despite his failure. Jesus tells him, "Feed my lambs," and drops the comparison in the second question. To Peter's relief the Lord accepts his confession and reinstates him with the words, "Tend my sheep." Peter's love for the Lord will be made manifest in his care for the Lord's flock. He had claimed devotion greater than the others and his willingness to die for Christ. As we will see, he will die for Christ. He will die a martyr's death for the glory of God. But he wasn't yet ready and had made his boast impulsively, no doubt sincerely, but not yet ready. This encounter with his resurrected Savior, the affirmation of his love, and his commission would prepare him for that day when he would give his life for Christ and the gospel which he faithfully preached. There would be a third question to probe more deeply Peter's love for Christ.

LOVE JESUS AS HE IS, NOT THE JESUS YOU WISH HIM TO BE

We are called to become like Jesus and follow him as he is. Yet we often are trying to make Jesus more like ourselves and follow a Jesus we have created in our own minds, a Jesus who is easier on us, less demanding. Peter had not wanted a crucified Lord. He and the other disciples wanted an earthly king and an earthly kingdom, not so unlike some Christians who have tried to bring into existence a kingdom or a Christian country which are not Christ's. Peter's initial relief at meeting Jesus around the fire must have been shaken when Jesus questioned him repeatedly. The unexpected repetitions of the Lord's question to Peter were to search him to the depths of his being. There are variations in the questions and the words translated "love," *agape* and *phileo*. Some commentators see in these words a difference between profound love and fondness. Yet there are times in the New Testament that these words are used interchangeably. Keep in mind that the conversation was most likely in Aramaic. The choice of words is John's and may actually reflect Jesus' tone of voice. One thing we do know—Christ's knowledge of Peter's heart and his love even when his actions have denied him. The third time there was no yes, only "Lord, you know everything" (v. 17). Jesus again said, "Feed my sheep."

The point of this encounter is to rid Peter of his old self-confidence and assertiveness that he expressed before the crucifixion. Peter really did love Jesus, and more than that he could not say. More than that was not necessary. He would no longer boast of what he would do or not do. His self-confidence was gone. The Lord accepted his declaration of love and restored him. Peter is told to take care of Jesus' flock. He was not placed in a position of exclusive authority over the church as the successor of Jesus and certainly was not appointed as ruler over the church. First Peter 5:1 shows how Peter understood his position as an elder among others, as a "fellow elder." Peter did have a unique role in founding the church as the principal spokesman on the Day of Pentecost (Acts 2:14). You see, Jesus not only predicted Peter's fall but Peter's recovery. "When you have turned again, strengthen your brothers" (Luke 22:32). His failure and restoration prepared him for ministry to others. Notice that Peter did not have to ask Jesus if he loved Peter. Peter knew. You should know how much he loves you.

YOUR FAILURE ITSELF DOES NOT DISQUALIFY YOU FROM SERVING THE LIVING CHRIST

Peter was grieved that Jesus asked the question a third time (v. 17). We should have sorrow when we fail or deny Christ by how we live or what we say. We should then look past the grief and by grace see a forgiving Savior who restores and refreshes his people. Our God is the God of second and third chances, and even more. That does not mean we take sin lightly or that there are not serious consequences that accompany disobedience or unfaithfulness. Yet whatever the failures of the past, Jesus restores Peter to a place of trust and a place of service. When you sin, when you fail or deny Christ, it might take time to demonstrate the reality of repentance. Your place of service might not be the same as before. Other qualities may be desirable, but love for Christ is indispensable and will be seen in your life and actions. Genuine love for Christ also leads to authentic service. There can be service in the form of activity without love. There cannot be love without service. Our failures and restoration likewise prepare us to minister to others, to understand their weaknesses because we are weak, to sympathize because we share in the human condition and the frailty of our flesh, to forgive because we have been forgiven, and to be gracious because we have experienced grace. We don't need to pretend that we are more spiritual than others and live on a higher level, that we are less often tempted, or that we have never failed. Your spiritual leaders are all flawed, but they should be committed to Christ and his word. In our own church we've had leaders who have been disqualified from leadership because of moral failure. We always sought repentance and restoration for them even if they no longer served in the same capacity. Failure does not disqualify you from living for Christ and serving him.

YOUR FUTURE IS IN THE HANDS OF THE LORD (REGARDLESS OF HOW AND WHEN YOUR LIFE ENDS)

There would come a time as Peter aged that he would be restrained, in some way no longer master of his movements. When he was young he dressed himself. The time would come, Jesus said, when "you will stretch out your hands, and another will dress you and carry you where you do not want to go" (v. 18). The phrase "stretch out your hands" appears to refer to crucifixion, although not all commentators agree.[1] Peter would be tied up as an old man and led away by "another," the one who ties up the condemned and leads him away to execution. By this death he would glorify God (v. 19). Peter lived for many years with the sentence of death on him yet accepted the cross of serving Christ and one day would be crucified upside down, according to tradition. By the time this Gospel was written Peter had already died and passed into glory. The obscurity of the saying was clarified by the event. God is glorified in those who lay down their lives for the name of Jesus. The shame of Peter's

1. Carson, *John*, 679.

denials was removed by a life of service ending in martyrdom. Criticize Peter if you will for his denial of Christ, but only if you have never found yourself in his place. We do not know "what kind of death" we shall have, but when the day comes it can most assuredly be for the glory of God. As Piper says, "The way we die reveals the worth of Christ in our hearts. Christ is magnified in my death when I am satisfied with him in my dying . . . Christ will be praised in my death if in my death he is prized above life."[2] Peter lived and served Christ with this knowledge of his death, not like a threatening sword of Damocles hanging over his head, but as a special promise and word of the assurance of Christ's loving care for him to the end.

Jesus has not called you to himself in order to live your life according to your will but according to his. Jesus said simply "Follow me!" (v. 19). Peter was to follow Christ in discipleship the remainder of his days. It is no less true for you and me today. "Follow him." Jesus asks you today, "Do you love me?" Why do you call him Lord, Lord, and do not do what he tells you? (Luke 6:46). In what way in your life are you not following Christ; what area of your life have you not allowed him to rule? Perhaps there are broken relationships for which you refuse to seek reconciliation. Perhaps there has been silence in the presence of those who need to hear a word from you, God's word through you. You may feel guilty at times because you are guilty. You may be guilty at times when you don't feel guilty. We can see what the Lord sees, our failures, and yet we see God's grace in Christ. We see forgiveness. We see our lives lived according to what he says and not according to our own ambitions. Simply say today, "Lord, I will follow you, in your strength, and by your grace, to the end, however and whenever the end comes." You may find yourself weary, worn out, troubled, ill, or nearing the end of your earthly sojourn. Paul tells us that "we who are in this [body] groan, being burdened" and that our mortality will be "swallowed up by life" (2 Cor 5: 4). Often recall these words and God's promise from 2 Corinthians, meditate on them, and remember that you are not home yet.

> 16 Therefore we do not lose heart. Even though our outward man
> is perishing, yet the inward man is being renewed day by day. 17
> For our light affliction, which is but for a moment, is working for
> us a far more exceeding and eternal weight of glory, 18 while we
> do not look at the things which are seen, but at the things which
> are not seen. For the things which are seen are temporary, but the
> things which are not seen are eternal.

2. Piper, *Don't Waste Your Life*, 68.

Bibliography

Annaud, Jean-Jacques, dir. *Enemy at the Gates*. Los Angeles: Mandalay Pictures, 2001.

Bock, Darrell L. *Luke*. Baker Exegetical Commentary on the New Testament 1. Grand Rapids, MI: Baker, 1994.

Bruce, F. F. *The Epistle to the Hebrews*. The New International Commentary on the New Testament. Grand Rapids, MI: Eerdmans, 1990.

Carson, D. A. *The Gospel According to John*. Grand Rapids, MI: Eerdmans, 1991.

Colman, Stephen M., and Todd M. Rester, eds. *Faith in the Time of Plague: Selected Writings from the Reformation and Post-Reformation*. Glenside, PA: Westminster Seminary Press, 2021.

Council on Foreign Relations. "Global Conflict Tracker." https://www.cfr.org/global-conflict-tracker/?category=us.

Dodd, C. H. *The Parables of the Kingdom*. New York: Scribner, 1961.

Drake, Nadia. "Jeff Bezos Reaches Space—A Small Step toward Big Spaceflight Dreams." *National Geographic* July 20, 2021. https://www.nationalgeographic.com/science/article/jeff-bezos-flies-to-space-on-blue-origin-rocket.

Early Church Texts. "Epistle to Diognetus - chapters 5–7." https://earlychurchtexts.com/public/epistle_to_diognetus.htm.

Ferguson, Sinclair B. *The Holy Spirit: Contours of Christian Theology*. Downers Grove, IL: InterVarsity, 1996.

Green, Joel B. *The Gospel of Luke*. Edited by Gordon D. Fee et al. The New International Commentary on the New Testament. Grand Rapids, MI: Eerdmans, 1997.

Gundry, Robert Horton. *Mark: A Commentary on His Apology for the Cross*. Grand Rapids, MI: Eerdmans, 1993.

Hauerwas, Stanley, and William H. Willimon. *Resident Aliens: Life in the Christian Colony*. Nashville: Abington, 2014.

Hendriksen, William. *Exposition of the Gospel According to Luke. New Testament Commentary*. Grand Rapids, MI: Baker Academic, 1978.

Hiebert, D. Edmond. *Mark: Portrait of a Servant*. Chicago: Moody, 1974.

———. *Second Timothy*. Chicago: Moody, 1959.

———. *The Thessalonian Epistles: A Call to Readiness*. Chicago: Moody, 1971.

James, Sharon. "Uncommon Wife of Revival." https://www.desiringgod.org/articles/uncommon-wife-of-revival.

Kistemaker, Simon J. *Exposition of the Acts of the Apostles. New Testament Commentary*. Grand Rapids, MI: Baker, 1990.

Lewis, C. S. *Mere Christianity*. San Francisco: Harper, 2001.

Lutzer, Erwin W. *Hitler's Cross*. Chicago: Moody, 1995.

Martel, Yann. *Life of Pi: A Novel*. Orlando: Harcourt, 2001.

Moo, Douglas J. *Galatians*. Baker Exegetical Commentary on the New Testament. Grand Rapids, MI: Baker Academic, 2013.

Morris, Edmund. *Edison*. New York: Random, 2019.

O'Brien, Peter T. *The Letter to the Ephesians*. The Pillar New Testament Commentary. Grand Rapids, MI: Eerdmans, 1999.

Packer, J. I. *Finishing Our Course with Joy: Guidance from God for Engaging with Aging*. Wheaton, IL: Crossway. 2014.

Pascal, Blaise. *Pensées*. Translated by W. F. Trotter. Mineola, NY: Dover, 2003.

Piper, John. "Declare His Glory Among the Nations." https://www.desiringgod.org/messages/declare-his-glory-among-the-nations.

———. *Desiring God: Meditations of a Christian Humanist*. Colorado Springs, CO: Multnomah, 2011.

———. *Don't Waste Your Life*. Wheaton, IL: Crossway, 2007.

———. "I Do Not Aspire to Be a 'Regular Guy.'" https://www.desiringgod.org/articles/i-do-not-aspire-to-be-a-regular-guy.

———. *Let the Nations Be Glad: The Supremacy of God in Missions*. 3rd ed. Grand Rapids, MI: Baker Academic, 2010.

———. "The Pleasure of God in His Son." https://www.desiringgod.org/messages/the-pleasure-of-god-in-his-son.

———. "Why Would God Create a Baby to Live for Two Minutes?" https://www.desiringgod.org/interviews/why-would-god-create-a-baby-to-live-for-two-minutes.

Rhodes, Jonty. *Man of Sorrows, King of Glory*. Wheaton, IL: Crossway, 2021.

Sample, Ian. "Stephen Hawking: 'There Is No Heaven; It's a Fairy Story.'" *The Guardian* May 15, 2011. https://www.theguardian.com/science/2011/may/15/stephen-hawking-interview-there-is-no-heaven.

Shibley, David, and Naomi Shibley. *The Smoke of a Thousand Villages*. Nashville: Thomas Nelson, 1989.

Silva, Moisés. *Philippians*. Baker Exegetical Commentary on the New Testament. Grand Rapids, MI: Baker, 1992.

Tate, Marvin E. *Psalms 51–100*. Word Biblical Commentary 20. Grand Rapids, MI: Zondervan, 2015.

Tolkien, J. R. R. *The Fellowship of the Ring*. New York: HarperCollins, 1991.

VanGemeren, William A. "Psalms." In *The Expositor's Bible Commentary: Psalms, Proverbs, Ecclesiastes, Song of Solomon*, edited by Frank Gæbelein, 5:5–880. Grand Rapids, MI: Zondervan, 1991.

Made in the USA
Las Vegas, NV
29 September 2022